The Lively Art of Writing
Developing Structure

The Lively Art of Writing

Developing Structure

LUCILE VAUGHAN PAYNE

Follett Publishing Company
Editorial Offices: Chicago, Illinois

Regional Offices: Chicago, Illinois
Atlanta, Georgia • Dallas, Texas
Sacramento, California • Warrensburg, Missouri

Contents

1

What Is an Essay?

Ever since the first cave dwellers discovered that they could draw arrows on the ground with pointed sticks or scratch designs on the walls of their caves with pieces of flint, human beings have been trying to communicate with one another by means of written symbols. Those ancient arrows may have served only to mark the direction taken by an unfriendly animal. The designs etched on the stone walls of a prehistoric family room may have represented no more than an instinctive effort at self-expression. But whatever their motives were when they began to make marks, those distant ancestors of ours were responding to a basic human urge—the urge to communicate. And although writing today is a far more complicated process, the basic urge behind every piece of writing remains the same: to communicate, to share knowledge and ideas and feelings, to say to the world "This is the way things are."

That is the purpose of all writing, whether the particular specimen is a newspaper account, a magazine article, a piece of fiction, a poem, or a letter. It is also the purpose of an essay.

An essay, however, is neither a mere record of fact nor a pure work of the imagination. The paper that you write for a history class, crowded with facts you have gathered from reference works, may look like an essay and could conceivably be one, but it probably isn't, no matter how carefully you have rewritten all the facts in your own words. Neither is the painstaking, step-by-step how-to paper, no matter how clear and precise; nor the description of a particular scene, no matter how accurate the details or how lyrical the language.

You have probably written hundreds of such compositions since you entered school, lumping them all together under that much-abused heading, "themes." You may even have called them essays. But they are seldom essays.

We usually think of essays as falling into one or the other of two broad groupings: formal essays and informal, or "familiar," essays. The root of the word *formal* is *form*. It means "shape," or the way something is put together or done. A formal essay is one that has a rather definite and readily recognized shape, one that follows a generally accepted pattern. By contrast, the familiar essay follows no specific form. Finding its subject almost anywhere, even in the most ordinary of everyday occurrences, it depends directly for its appeal upon the craft and artistry of the writer. The subject of this book is the formal essay because, of the two, it is the easier to analyze and understand, and for most of us it is more immediately useful.

Don't be put off by the word *formal*. It is not a synonym for *dull*. The formal essay is not by its own nature stiff and straightlaced and heavy, nor should it be. If it is, blame the writer, not the form. A formal essay requires the same life-giving ingredients that all writing must have if it is to hold the interest of a reader.

What, then, is an essay?

➤ *An essay is the written expression of one person's opinion on one particular subject.* At its best, an essay blends fact with imagination, knowledge with feeling, never giving itself over wholly to one or the other. But its purpose is always the same: to express an opinion.

10

Essays will differ in quality and in kind, in length, in style, in subject. They will range from the very simple to the exceedingly complex. But in the final analysis, every essay expresses a personal opinion. This is the critical difference between the essay and the expository theme or the mere report. An essay does not merely record facts or recount experiences; it registers the author's *opinion* of these facts and experiences. In other words, *it interprets their meaning*.

That's why the study of the essay form is so rewarding. Too often students let themselves become machines—collecting information without giving it any real thought, then reproducing it (rather like computer printouts) for the teacher's inspection at exam time. But students are not machines when they write essays; they are human beings—selecting, judging, evaluating, interpreting, expressing not only what they know but what they *are*. Thus every attempted essay is a kind of voyage toward self-discovery.

The methods an essayist may use to express an opinion vary enormously, depending to some extent upon subject matter but to an even greater extent upon the author's particular view of life or way of looking at things. Opinions can be put forward seriously or humorously, scientifically or imaginatively, formally or informally. They may be stated explicitly in some kinds of essays, implied subtly in others. The main thing to remember is simply that opinion is always present. It is at the heart of every essay.

Obviously, then, you must have an opinion before you can write an essay. Therefore you need to know exactly what an opinion is, how to arrive at it, how to judge its value. Before you can reach an opinion, however, you must decide upon a subject, for opinions exist not in a vacuum but always in relation to particular subjects. So we begin our search for opinion with the question, "What makes a good subject?"

Subjects for Essays

"What shall I write about?" This is the universal student question, a kind of midnight howl of anguish, loudest and most hopeless the night before an essay assignment is due.

11

Yet of all the problems an essayist must tackle, the choice of subject is in some ways the simplest. For the choice is almost limitless. You can write an essay about literally anything—friendship or fashions, Puritanism or politics, shoes or ships or sealing wax. You can even write an essay about essays. Any subject that the human mind has ever considered or investigated or wondered about provides material for an essay.

° The only requirement is that the writer know enough about the subject to arrive at some kind of reasonable opinion.

What constitutes "knowing enough"? Certainly some ideas and experiences are so familiar to all of us that it can be safely said that everybody "knows enough." These are the commonplaces of human existence—friendship, family relationships, growing up, eating and sleeping, working and playing. The list is almost endless; it is simply the stuff of everyday life. And it provides an immense body of material for essays, all of it immediately and equally available to any writer. This is the stuff of the familiar essay.

"Knowing enough" to write about some subjects, however, requires familiarity with more specialized knowledge. An essay on Puritanism, for example—or Swahili or internal-combustion engines or sailboating or microbiology—would be meaningless unless its author had a knowledge of the subject beyond the mere accidental contact of everyday life. Every student knows a little about Puritanism, if only that Puritans wore tall black hats and took a rather dim view of sin. But Puritanism is an idea with a specific place in history, an idea that has had enormous significance in shaping our society. To write about it without adequate information or understanding would be to invite ridicule. It is possible to write an adequate essay on a topic like friendship without being in command of a large body of facts, but it is not possible to do so on a topic like Puritanism. This, or any other specialized subject, requires solid information.

Fortunately, such information is easily and quickly accessible. The reference shelves of the library brim with facts and expert opinion about everything under the sun. You can find out about literally anything that interests you; your own interests, in fact, will guide you faster than anything else toward a suitable essay topic. Even a mild interest has a way of taking fire when you give it the fuel of facts. And once you start reading, you will soon be in command of enough information to question, to compare, to make judgments of your own. By reading what others have already written about a subject that interests you, you will come very quickly into possession of specialized knowledge.

As a matter of fact, it's likely that you already have far more specialized knowledge at your fingertips than you realize. Since your first day of school, you have been exposed to subject matter. Inevitably, you have opinions about it. Any subject listed on your transcript—particularly any subject that has awakened in you a real interest, or even a real antagonism—provides you with essay material. The subject may be as academic as Latin or as practical as auto mechanics; if you have studied it, you will "know enough" to write an essay based on what you have learned.

Hobbies provide another rich source of specialized knowledge. Your friend down the block who loves to tinker and somehow manages to fix almost anything mechanical that's out of order, the neighbor who raises tropical fish, the amateur photographer, the budding rock guitarist, the jazz buff—all these hobbyists will "know enough" about their favorite subjects to write about them with authority. Each has a solid body of information about his or her special interest. All have plenty of ideas about their own particular love, and all are prepared to explain and defend those ideas with confidence. Or indeed with passion. (Have you ever listened to a true sports car buff warm to the merits of double overhead cams? Or heard a rock devotee extol the virtues of a particular recording group, demonstrating just why it deserves to be at the very top of absolutely everyone's rating list?) Dedicated hobbyists almost invariably equip themselves with plenty of information and experience to back up their opinions.

And that, incidentally, tends to make the essay based on specialized knowledge much easier to write than the essay based on a familiar idea or commonplace experience. The author's opinion is an *informed* opinion. To put it bluntly, the author knows what he or she is talking about. What passes for opinion in relation to familiar ideas and experiences is all too often merely prejudice or habit or some fuzzy generalization that the author "feels" to be true. With the formal essay, you cannot rely on mere feeling. You must dig through all sorts of vague impressions and obscure convictions in order to isolate a real opinion—a firmly held, specific, reasonable statement of what you *think* rather than a foggy declaration of what you feel.

Regardless of the subject you choose to write about, you must have an *opinion* about it. What you know about it is important. What you feel about it is important. But more important than either is your *opinion* of what you know or feel, your interpretation of it. That is where your essay must begin.

What Is an Opinion, and How Do You Reach It?

Most of us use the word *opinion* very loosely. We tend to claim as opinions all sorts of prejudices, sentiments, platitudes, and vague convictions. But a genuine opinion strong enough to support the structure of an essay must meet certain specifications, all of them clearly laid out in this definition:

> *opinion:*
> a belief not based on absolute certainty or positive knowledge but on what seems true, valid, or probable to one's own mind; what one thinks; judgment.

You could not find a tool better suited to your purposes than this definition. Test any opinion against it and you will know immediately whether you have chosen a valid essay topic. It will make clear the difference between opinion and fact; the failure to make this distinction is perhaps the commonest error among student writers.

Is your opinion based on absolute certainty? On positive knowledge? Can you prove beyond all reasonable doubt that it is true? Then it is not an opinion at all. It is a fact—or an observation so commonplace that it has the status of fact.

Facts must be converted into opinions before they can serve as essay topics. It is a fact, for example, that the population of the United States is now about 230 million. The figure is a matter of record; it can be proved. To convert such a fact into a suitable essay topic you must ask yourself what it means; you must *judge* it, reach an opinion about it. Your judgment might be that the character of our national life is changing as a result of our increased population, or that immediate research is necessary to guarantee a food supply in the future, or that new ways of educating young people must be found if public education is to survive. Thus, by making a judgment, you have converted a fact into an opinion—and you have a valid essay topic.

Sometimes an opinion must be discarded as an essay topic because it is so generally accepted that it has the status of fact. Suppose, for example, that you choose to write an essay about friendship. You may come up with an opinion like this: "Friendship is an important human relationship." Fact or opinion? You may claim it is opinion because it cannot be scientifically or statistically proved. Yet it is a poor opinion for essay purposes because it is not in any real sense subject to argument. For all practical purposes, it is a fact. Only an extremely gifted and original writer could hope to make it interesting. In the hands of a beginner, such a commonplace is almost certain to be overpoweringly dull.

Opinions in this category must be converted, as facts must be converted, into sharply defined judgments. The best way to convert a commonplace into an interesting, thought-provoking essay topic is to bombard it with questions: "Is real friendship possible between a boy and a girl? between parents and their children? between people of different races or colors or religions?" Answer Yes or No to any of these questions (or to a hundred others like them) and you will

15

have made a judgment about human relations. You will have committed yourself to an *opinion,* and will therefore have provided yourself with an essay topic.

This is perhaps the simplest method of arriving at an opinion. But to uncover what might prove to be a more interesting, or even more significant, essay topic, you need to pry further and ask yourself "how," "why," and "what" questions: "*How* can parents and children learn to be friends? *Why* is friendship sometimes difficult to achieve with people of a different race, color, or religion? *What* can one do to understand and break through barriers to friendship?" These are all questions that require a complete statement as an answer. They are, as a matter of fact, the same questions you are likely to ask yourself eventually if you develop an essay from the simple yes-or-no question. The point is that in either case the answer is an *opinion.*

The more questions you ask yourself, the better. Questions force you down from a great cloudy mass of ideas to the solid ground of real thought. You will learn quickly to recognize the questions that are pointless, that require too much information, or that simply can't be answered in the brief space of an essay. And you will discover, as you formulate and answer questions, a great many opinions that you have never before put into words—which is another way of saying that you have never really known what you really think. Don't snatch the first answer that occurs to you and call off the search. Keep asking questions. When you come up with an answer so interesting and challenging and so right that it strikes you as a personal discovery, you can be sure you have moved into the real territory of the essayist.

The same process applies to more academic subjects. Your first thought about Puritanism, for example, might be that "Puritanism was a strong influence on early New England society." But this is not an opinion. It's a fact. You can prove it without the slightest difficulty. Therefore, it's a poor essay topic. Bombard it with questions that can be answered with *opinions,* and you begin collecting good essay topics: Did Puritan thought and values slip across the New England

16

borders and influence the thought and values of Americans elsewhere? If so, to what extent? Is Puritanism dead, or is it still an active force in American life? Can it explain some of our attitudes today? How? As questions and answers multiply, your problem is no longer one of finding an essay topic but of choosing the most interesting one among many.

What Makes an Opinion Interesting?

You will quickly discover that certain opinions you reach seem more interesting than others. Certainly your own enthusiasm for your subject has something to do with this. All of us write best about the subjects we like best. Or you may find one topic more interesting than another simply because you have done a better job of putting it into words; some happy turn of phrase has given it spice and character. But more effective than anything else in arousing interest in an opinion is *opposition*. If a substantial number of people disagree with your views on a subject, you may be sure that your views will excite interest.

This is the real explanation for the weakness as an essay topic of an opinion like "Friendship is important." It falls flat because nobody of reasonable intelligence would dream of challenging it. Readers simply are not interested in an opinion so obviously and demonstrably true. You could write some kind of paper about it, of course, but who would want to read it? Your mother, maybe. Or your best friend. But even they might have difficulty disguising their yawns.

Conflict, say the journalists, is one of the most important of the ingredients that go to make up what they term "news." The more significant the conflict—that is, the more directly it touches the lives of everyone—the greater the news value. People become interested. They project *themselves* into the conflict and begin to take sides. Something similar happens when a reader becomes involved in a good essay.

No argument, no essay. It is almost as simple as that. For every essay, in the final analysis, is an argument. It represents one side in a conflict between points of view. It is one

17

writer pitting one opinion against every other opinion on the same subject. The stronger the opposition, the hotter the argument—and the greater the interest. Make certain, therefore, when you choose an opinion to defend, that it is an opinion likely to rub a few people the wrong way. "Pigs are smarter than horses"—say that and immediately everybody who ever cherished an Old Paint, a Chief, or a Pete, real or imagined, will be clamoring for equal time. Opposition—therefore interest—is guaranteed.

But opposition alone is not enough. Value judgments of the this-is-better-than-that variety always have a clear-cut opposition, but they have serious limitations. For one thing, they can easily deteriorate into meaningless I'm-right-you're-wrong exchanges that prove nothing and convince nobody.

With many subjects, you need only take a position. For example, the moment you say "Students should be required to do more writing," you will almost certainly outrage every student who considers the creation of even one sentence a labor beyond endurance. Say "The movie that should win this year's Oscar is *The Purple Monster*," and you will draw the immediate fire of the moviegoer who is certain that *The Polka-Dot Monster* should be the winner. Even a difference in interpretation can provide the necessary element of controversy: "*The Purple Monster* gave an accurate portrayal of the typical American husband" will stir up everybody who considered the movie a vicious attack upon American men.

Examining the Opposition

As you begin to shape opinions for essays, force yourself to question your position by considering carefully everything that can be said in favor of a strongly different opinion. If you believe that students should do *more* writing, consider all the reasons for doing *less* writing. If you want to demonstrate that pigs are smarter than horses, look for all the reasons others may have for being certain that horses are smarter than pigs. Always make yourself thoroughly aware of every

18

argument that might be used against your particular point of view.

Such careful consideration of every side of an issue occasionally has the surprising result of causing you to change your mind. Splendid. You still have an opinion—merely a different one. And you are likely to be an even stronger advocate of your new opinion than you were of the old. But even if your first opinion is as strong as ever, your tour through opposition territory will have made you more aware of the strengths and weaknesses of your position, thus giving you a better idea of how to defend it.

An opinion, after all, is simply one person's idea of the truth, his or her guess at the meaning of facts or ideas or circumstances. Suppose a study of your town reveals that the crime rate has gone up in the past few years. X, after considering the facts, makes one judgment ("The town has an inadequate police force."); Y makes a different judgment ("The churches or the schools are failing in their responsibilities."); Z arrives at still another judgment ("The town is in the hands of corrupt politicians."). Each is able to defend one particular judgment with honest conviction.

Which judgment is correct? Which represents the final truth? Nobody knows, for truth is not something that can be weighed, measured, labeled, and conveniently stored for future reference. But the public, after weighing the arguments of X, Y, and Z, will accept as truth the opinion that is supported by the most evidence, that is the most logical, the fairest, the most clearly stated, the most persuasive.

Even so with an essay. You cannot expect your opinion to be subject to scientific proof. Your purpose is to examine and to persuade, not to prove, and the strength of your essay will depend upon how carefully you examine the evidence and how well you persuade a reader to agree with your particular view. Every opinion that you are considering as a potential essay topic, then, should be checked against two questions. Ask yourself: "Can a valid argument be made against it? Can I defend it *logically* against this argument?"

If you can answer Yes to both these questions, you can be

reasonably sure that you are on the trail of an interesting essay topic.

A gifted and original writer can, of course, present almost any idea with such fresh insight and in such beguiling language that the resulting essay will be interesting even without a clearly defined opposing point of view. Sometimes the purpose of an essay is simply to arouse interest where none existed before. In that case, the writer must overcome the roughest opposition of all—pure apathy, the reluctance of most readers to bother with anything that doesn't rouse their instinct to take sides.

You will find it much easier, on the whole, to write your first essays on topics that have a clearly defined opposition. Get the hang of that process first, then you can move on to the subtleties.

Believe What You Say

A good essay topic will always be subject to argument. But the argument must be honest and intelligent. You can arouse temporary interest, of course, with an opinion that contradicts all logic or established facts ("Friendship is unimportant." "Puritanism had no real influence, even in New England."). But a bizarre opinion manufactured simply to attract attention is an obvious and silly device. Worse yet, it's dishonest. You are naturally eager to escape dullness, but if you must make a choice between a dull topic and a dishonest one, by all means choose dullness. Dullness in writing can be cured. Dishonesty can't. Honesty is quite literally the best policy for the essayist; it's the only policy, in fact, that works.

So believe in your opinion. This does not mean that you should reject summarily every opinion that doesn't get your immediate and wholehearted approval. To the contrary. Ideas that don't get your immediate approval are the very ones you should look at most closely. You cannot, after all, claim to have arrived at an opinion until you have examined, thoroughly and fairly, every legitimate argument against it.

But once you have done this, you can be secure in your belief, and it will help guide you between the Scylla of dullness and the Charybdis of mendacity.

Summary

Pick a subject, examine everything you know about it, arrive at an honest opinion. That probably sounds easy. It isn't. But it represents at least half the work involved in writing an essay. And most of it you can do without touching a pencil. The first maxim of the essayist could hardly be made clearer: *Think before you write.*

Never sit down to write about any essay subject until you have thought about it long enough and hard enough to have an opinion about it—an opinion that you believe in and want to share, one that you can defend logically and honestly. Most essay-writing skills are relatively easy to learn, but it is pointless to learn them—in fact, you will find it almost impossible to learn them—unless you have learned the first rule, the unbreakable rule, of essay writing: *Opinion always comes first.*

And of course it comes first because as soon as you have an opinion, you have something to say. That's the important thing: Have something to say. Then you can learn how to say it. The skills come easily when you have a purpose for learning them. Have something to say—and if you really want to be heard, nothing can stop you from learning how to say it well.

QUESTIONS

1. What is the difference between opinion and fact?
2. How important are facts in an essay?
3. Is one opinion as good as another? Explain your answer.
4. Assuming that the writer has an adequate background in the subject, would American foreign policy be a good general subject for an essay? Why or why not?

5. The titles below are grouped around particular subjects. Which title in each group would make the best essay topic? Why?

    a. Sewing as a Hobby
       Clothes You Make Yourself
       Sewing Is Suddenly "In"
       How to Make a Pleated Skirt

    b. How TV Surveys Are Conducted
       The Ten Worst TV Shows of the Year
       National News Coverage on TV
       The Newest TV Technology

    c. *Moby Dick*
       The Symbolism in *Moby Dick*
       The Character of Ahab in *Moby Dick*
       Moby Dick, America's Greatest Novel

6. What is the chief difference between a typical term paper and an essay?

ASSIGNMENT

1. Write a one-sentence opinion based on each of the subjects below.

drugs	grades	politics
energy crisis	jobs	television news
environment	mass transit	women's rights

2. Choose one of your opinions, and list at least three facts that will support it.

3. Write a one-sentence opinion that is exactly opposite to yours, and list three facts that will support it. (Your facts must be convincing even though you may not agree with the opinion.)

4. Write at least two paragraphs using all the material you have written for 2 and 3 above (the two opinions and both sets of facts). You must reword the material to suit your purpose, but be sure to use all of it in some way, relating the paragraphs clearly so that the reader will understand why you favor one opinion instead of the other.

1. Look up the following words in a dictionary. Find a synonym and an antonym for each word. List them under the separate headings *Words, Synonyms,* and *Antonyms.*

adequate	bizarre	platitude
antagonism	explicit (ly)	subtleties
apathy	maxim	valid

2. In your opinion, what is the meaning of the term "value judgment"? Use a specific example to illustrate.

3. In the chapter you have just read, the following phrase appears: "the Scylla of dullness and the Charybdis of mendacity." Look up the meanings of *mendacity, Scylla,* and *Charybdis.* Find the text sentence containing the phrase, and copy the complete sentence. Then explain what the sentence means.

2

From Opinion to Thesis

In Chapter 1, the word *opinion* appeared over and over. The repetition was deliberate. Its purpose was to impress permanently upon your mind the need to have an opinion on your subject before you begin to write an essay.

Now it is time to take a closer look at that word *opinion*. It's a rather broad term. When you say, "It looks like rain," you are expressing an opinion—but it is not an opinion likely to inspire an essay. As a budding essayist, you need a word that more precisely describes the particular kind of opinion represented in an essay. That word is *thesis*.

The thesis of your essay is your opinion boiled down to one arguable statement. Everything else in the essay depends on your thesis, for the whole purpose of your essay is to explain and clarify and defend and illustrate that thesis—and thus to persuade the reader of its truth. The thesis is, you might say, pure extract of essay; it is the *one major point* you want to make, with everything else stripped away. It is a straight, unadorned statement of the opinion you have chosen as your essay topic. You arrive at this opinion through a process of selection that is the very essence of thought—the narrowing of a broad subject to one specific judgment.

You have already had a glimpse of this process with topics like friendship and Puritanism in Chapter 1. You know generally that what you must do is to pick your way through a great mass of ideas and impressions and finally to close in on your subject. Now let's watch the process at work.

Closing In on Your Thesis

No hard-and-fast rule can cover all the methods of closing in. Too much depends upon the kind of subject you have chosen and upon your own way of thinking about things. But certain general principles can guide you, as you will see in the examples that follow.

Let's assume that you have been asked to work out a thesis based on one of the subjects below.

elective courses	television
sports	crime
popular slang	spending for elections
jobs for teenagers	energy conservation

The topics in the column on the right suggest questions or problems that concern everyone, regardless of age or occupation. Undoubtedly you know something about all of them. It may even be that you have some rather decided notions about one or two. But you would need a great deal more than that to write knowledgeably and intelligently about any of these topics. All four would require a great deal of research.

The topics in the column on the left are much closer to home; they are directly related to the student world in which you live and work five days a week for much of the year. Consequently, a paper based upon any one of these topics should not present too serious a challenge. Of the four, "jobs for teenagers" would make the greatest demands upon you, extending as it does into all sorts of social and economic byways outside the school. But since you are not yet writing the full essay and are concerned for the present only with learning how to develop a thesis, let's begin with this topic. If you can formulate a good thesis on jobs, you should have no trouble doing it with a topic less demanding. Moreover, it's a subject that has enormous significance for many students (and perhaps even more for recent graduates).

The Five-Step Process

The process of finding a thesis consists mainly of, first, finding out what you know about a subject and, second, determining your opinion of it based upon what you know. To do that, you should take these five basic steps:

1. Take inventory.

Since finding a thesis is a process of narrowing your subject to one specific idea—one opinion—you must first take inventory of what you know about the demand for jobs among teenagers and the job market open to them. So, how much do you know?

From personal experience or from friends, you are sure to have accumulated a large store of information. You know who of your acquaintances have jobs and who do not. You have heard from those who want a job but don't know how to go about securing one and from those who have "looked everywhere" but somehow just cannot find an opening. You know firsthand or from friends where the tips on jobs come from. You know how much your school and community are doing to help young people find work. You have heard or read the national statistics on teenage unemployment. You have seen what it has meant when someone you know has found a job. Or has failed to find one.

But you know something else, and it is probably the most important item in your inventory: you know the reasons that students usually give for wanting to earn money.

> I'm expected to buy my own clothes, or at least some of them.
>
> I need to help out at home.
>
> I just want a job.

I'm tired of being treated like a child.

I'm tired of being completely dependent on someone else.

I want to start living on my own.

The above is a mere sampling. When you have carefully inventoried your entire stock of information, you are ready for the next step.

2. Ask questions.

Look over your inventory and ask yourself questions. You may come up with something like this:

    A. Why is unemployment highest among teenagers?

    B. Why is unemployment among teenagers highest among minorities in the large cities?

    C. Whose responsibility is it to help teenagers find jobs?

You can think of other and probably better questions, but these will do for present purposes. You can get started toward a thesis, perhaps several, with what you have here.

The answer to Question A is too obvious to concern you for long. It's the old chicken-or-egg riddle all over again. You need experience to get a job but you must first have a job to get experience. Furthermore, older people got to the jobs before you, exercising the same advantage over you and your friends that you will hold over your younger brothers and sisters when their time comes to go job hunting.

Question B reminds us that the topic we are considering is extremely complicated. Almost any answer could be a thesis. But to give a sensible answer, you would need an enormous amount of information about the social and economic make-up of urban America. So let it pass for now. It may be one you will want to take on later.

Question C (Whose responsibility is it to help teenagers find jobs?) looks promising. So put it to the test.

Assuming that it is almost always best to start with the

27

familiar, start with your personal situation. Are you responsible, at least in part? Common sense dictates the answer to that one: yes, at least in part. You know, for example, that almost any kind of job in today's world—from waiting tables to running your own business—requires the ability to read, write, and compute. The responsibility for learning these skills is obviously yours, and yours only. Therefore, *some* of the responsibility for finding a job is yours.

So, you try that idea out as a thesis:

> I am partly responsible for finding myself a job.

Is it a thesis? Not really. A thesis needs to express an opinion worth arguing about. Nobody would give you an argument on a statement as obviously true as this one.

You might try to give it a more argumentative edge by changing it to this:

> I alone am responsible for finding myself a job.

Anything wrong with that? Yes. It simply isn't true. Very few people can create jobs for themselves. And one person alone cannot always know where jobs are to be found. So it is conceivable that you might prepare yourself extremely well to earn a living yet still be unable to find work. Last but not least, in both these trial-thesis sentences, you have switched emphasis. The topic is no longer "jobs for teenagers"; it's yourself.

At this point, you may want to ask yourself a further question: "If I alone can't shoulder the full responsibility, who shares it with me?"

You are getting much, much closer. Somewhere in one of the answers to that question lies a clue to a solid and sensible thesis—one you can handle. But before you settle firmly on anything, you need to stop and mull over what you have done so far, keeping in mind this final question about responsibility. Your awareness of that question may help you understand your thesis better when you finally decide upon one.

28

3. *Look for relationships.*

Turn to your inventory and consider again the ɪ students most often give for wanting jobs. Look especially at the last three items. (I'm tired of being treated like a child. I'm tired of being completely dependent on someone else. I want to start living on my own.) What may they suggest? Perhaps they suggest that for young people a job has a special value, a value beyond money: a real job means that adults now recognize that you are no longer a child. That you are, in fact, now one of them—an adult.

This is a thesis of sorts. If valid, it underscores how important it is that young people be able to find employment. It states a point you would want to make somewhere along the way if you were to attempt a full essay on the present topic. But does it strike at the heart of the problem under examination, jobs for teenagers? Not quite. But it's getting close.

Consider this: adults know that it is not in their interest to hold you in childhood forever, to deny you jobs, to bar your way into their world. They recognize that such a course of action would reduce society to a shambles very quickly. The country's entire economic and political structure would come tumbling down. The human instinct for survival makes even the thought of such delayed adulthood absurd. Does a thesis lurk in that idea?

> It is in society's interest, unless society wishes to self-destruct, to conduct the young into the adult world in a progressive and orderly fashion.

Is this, finally, the thesis you are looking for?

Sorry. It's too broad. Your main concern, jobs for teenagers, would get lost in an essay built on so broad a base. Moreover, it states a position that very few would want to argue against. Lay it aside for the time being. But keep it in mind. It's a point worth making somewhere along the line.

29

4. Ask the yes-or-no question.

Remember your earlier question? "If I alone can't shoulder the full responsibility, who shares it with me?" Now ask yourself this: "Does society share responsibility for helping young people find jobs?"

If you accept the argument that it is in the interest of society to help bring young people into the adult world, of course your answer is Yes. If society has something to gain, it seems reasonable to assume that it should take on some of the responsibility.

Now you are getting near the heart of the matter. Your answer to the yes-or-no question has provided you with a temporary working thesis:

> Society shares a responsibility for helping young people find jobs.

But this is a working thesis only, not a final one. The trouble with it is that no one—perhaps not even you—knows exactly what it means. Suppose an opponent argues that society is already assuming much of the responsibility and you respond with something like this: "What? What's it doing? You tell me who is doing anything that really means anything." You would finally be on the right track (*who* should be doing *what*), but you have reached the point only because you have been forced to it by your opponent. In short, your opponent has succeeded in taking your thesis and your essay away from you because your language had been too general and therefore too vague. You can't let that happen.

To prevent it, you need to do something about the words *society* and *responsibility*. They are foggy terms—too big, general, and unwieldy to transmit a precise meaning. You need to be more specific, more concrete, more exact, so that you and your readers are absolutely sure of the point you are trying to make. That's the final step you must take.

5. Qualify and limit.

Qualifying and limiting are almost the same thing. To qualify, you focus on the exact point you wish to defend,

30

making it precise, accurate, and reasonable. For example, a statement like "Everyone knows that" must be qualified because if one single person does not know, the statement is false. You qualify the statement by expressing as accurately as you can *who* knows or *how many* know. To limit, you whittle your subject down to a size you can defend and control. (You are still operating with only a working thesis, remember.)

So here you are, with those two big generalizations, "society" and "responsibility." Society consists of all of us and of all the groups and organizations and institutions— family, government, church, labor union, and so on—that we have established to express ourselves, look after our needs, and carry out our wishes. And *responsibility,* as you are using it here, suggests obligation, an obligation to help in the achievement of some goal.

With this in mind, you could rephrase your working thesis to something like this:

> The family, government, church, school, labor union, . . . all have an obligation to help achieve the goal of finding jobs for teenagers.

The amount of work that the defense of such a thesis would require is beyond all reason. You are not, after all, planning to write a book. And in any case, you wouldn't want to admit to the authorship of a statement so clumsy.

"Tell me who is doing anything that really means anything."

These words were forced upon you a few paragraphs back. Now at last you are ready to speak for yourself by revealing *who,* in your opinion, *should be doing what* to help teenagers find jobs. You can locate your "who" in your definition of society. Let us say that it is the school, an institution very familiar to you. You believe that schools should be doing more. More *what? What* do you think that schools ought to be doing? You are being asked, remember, to be so specific that no reasonably intelligent person can fail to understand what you have in mind.

31

You know that the state operates an employment service available to anyone seeking employment. You may or may not be aware that colleges and universities, too, have placement services that help their graduates find jobs.

Why, you wonder, wouldn't a placement service work equally well in high schools? It needn't be nearly as elaborate as those in colleges and universities. It could simply specialize in the kinds of jobs students and recent graduates would be qualified to fill. It could be located in the school, in familiar surroundings where students would have no call to feel uncertain or afraid. It might even be used in some way to teach. Ideas and possibilities and whys and why-nots race through your head. You see visions. You see a thesis.

> High schools should establish placement services to help students and recent graduates find jobs.

But look carefully at what you have discovered. Common sense tells us that what may be needed or may work in Cleveland, Ohio, may not be needed or may not work in Burns, Oregon. Different communities present different problems and different opportunities. Common sense also tells us that it would be foolish to propose something for everyone that, for all we know, may already exist in some school districts. So common sense suggests one further qualification: substitute the name of your particular school or school district for the more general term "high schools." You will thus be staking your claim on familiar ground.

> The Mira E. Schwirtz High School [or District X2] should establish a placement service to help students and recent graduates find jobs.

And there you have it. You have completed the five-step process, and you now have a thesis that you can work with. Is it the only thesis possible on this topic? Certainly not. If it were, no one could legitimately claim to have any other opinion on the subject, and of course that's not so. Given your information and the questions you asked yourself, is this the only thesis you could have come up with? Again, no.

You could have answered some of your own questions quite differently. You might have reached different conclusions. You might have reached many of the same conclusions but have offered a different solution. So let's say simply that the thesis as it now stands represents your considered opinion based upon what you know and understand at this time about the problems young people have finding jobs.

Defending Your Thesis

To defend your thesis intelligently, you need to be aware of the opinions others might hold and of all the arguments they might gather to attack your point of view—in this case, a definite proposal for a course of action that will affect at least some of those attackers. Opposing arguments will range from the very broad to specific counterproposals, or antitheses.* They are certain to include arguments like the following:

> Such a plan simply will not work.
>
> It would cost too much.
>
> It is the responsibility of the schools to train students for jobs, not to find jobs for them.
>
> The state employment service is the best agency for helping teenagers find jobs.
>
> The reason many teenagers cannot find employment is that they are not properly trained.
>
> Forced retirement of older workers will open the job market for teenagers.

And you can expect many, many others.

Suggestions for defending your thesis are already at hand. They lie in the process you followed just now as you closed in on your thesis. Your notes on the five-step process provide a rough outline of at least a part of your defense. To complete it, you must examine carefully every argument that may be

---

Antithesis is a word you should know. It means, literally, "against thesis," as you can probably guess by its prefix. But the pronunciation is tricky. The accent falls on the second syllable, and that *i* is short: an-TITH-uh-sis.

used against you. You may find that you don't know enough, that you have to collect more information and to rethink some of your conclusions. You may even change your mind about your own thesis so laboriously arrived at. But you cannot, after all, claim to have arrived at a valid judgment on any question until you have examined all the arguments that can be used against you.

So always look very closely and objectively at views opposed to your own. If you do this, you may be forced to concede a point here and there, to limit your thesis a little more strictly—but this merely leads to greater accuracy in presenting your view. And then you are in a stronger position than ever to write your essay. You can defend your thesis with real conviction.

A Subject on the Lighter Side

We began our discussion of finding a thesis with "jobs for teenagers" because it is an important subject and because it presents some life-size problems. Now let's take a look at a topic less complicated: "sports." What, that again? Yes, that again, and for excellent reasons, the chief one being its familiarity.

Although we listed qualifying and limiting as the fifth step in the closing-in process, you would probably need to start qualifying at the outset with a subject as broad as sports. This in itself makes a point you want to remember: You need not always take the five steps in order. They may come in almost any order, depending upon the nature of the subject and what you know about it.

Other than the facts that they are usually competitive in some way and that they are supposed to be enjoyable, sports vary so much that what is true of one may not be at all true of another. You find little similarity between basketball and baseball and less between boxing and golf. Football and fishing are about as far apart as war and peace. Therefore, the only sensible course is to limit the topic to one sport, using others, if need be, for comparison and contrast.

34

Suppose you are one of a rapidly growing number of soccer fans. You love the sport, and you believe that eventually it will challenge football for the hearts of people who want to play and for the dollars and applause of those who prefer to look on. Now you want to convince your friends of its thrills and its future. The opening round of your bout with a skeptic might go something like this:

You: Soccer is wonderful.

Skeptic: Soccer is a bore. Football is wonderful.
(All emotion; no appeal to reason.)

You: Soccer is the ideal sport for the person who likes to play and for the person who prefers to watch.

Skeptic: Football is the ideal sport for the person who likes to play and for the person who prefers to watch.
(Still emotion. Next, you'll be calling each other names.)

You: Soccer is an economical, continuous-action sport with far fewer physical limitations and hazards than football.

Skeptic: Soccer does not provide the hard-hitting contact of football, something that both fans and players enjoy.
(Points too close to the factual.)

You: Soccer is becoming increasingly popular and will eventually become more popular than football because of the advantages it offers everybody—players, fans, sponsors or owners.

Skeptic: Football is so firmly fixed in American sports traditions and habits that it will never lose its popularity to soccer.
(Closer, but both suggest supporting arguments not needed in the thesis.)

You: Soccer appears destined to surpass football in popularity in the United States.

Skeptic: Football must inevitably win any long-term popularity contest with soccer in the United States.
(Final thesis: the specific opinion you wish to argue.)

Notice that as the thesis sentences change, they change in only one major respect: *they become more specific.* Your opinion of soccer in the final version, for example, is basically no different from the opinion you expressed in the first version—quite obviously you still approve of it, even as your friend still prefers football. But the sweeping generalizations of "wonderful" and "a bore" have given way in each thesis to a very specific statement that points toward a reasonable and informed discussion rather than a mere expression of prejudice.

Furthermore, you and your opponent still have plenty of room under either final thesis to bring up any of the points you might have brought up under earlier versions. You will emphasize the "advantages," whatever you believe them to be, while your friend will dwell upon the solid position football has been able to build for itself over the last century. Increased accuracy in thesis does not necessarily limit argument; it simply improves organization.

Summary

Every essay is an opinion, but not every opinion is a good essay topic. It is a good topic only if it can be boiled down to one arguable statement about one major point. This statement is called a thesis. No matter what your essay is based upon, *you must have a thesis.* Formulating that thesis requires a great deal of hard thought, but you can make the task easier by following the basic pattern outlined in this chapter.

After you have worked out a firm thesis, you will know precisely what it is you want to say—and that is the first long step on the path toward better writing.

QUESTIONS

1. What is the difference between opinion and thesis?
2. What is the five-step process for narrowing a general subject to a thesis?

3. What is the value of the yes-or-no question?
4. Why is qualification of a thesis important?

ASSIGNMENT

At the top of a sheet of paper, write the name of some subject in which you are now enrolled. Then do the following:

1. Write at least five statements of fact about the subject.
2. Write at least two yes-or-no questions that occur to you in relation to these facts.
3. Write a thesis based on one of the questions.
4. Write an antithesis. (If your antithesis is not valid, write a new thesis. Keep trying until you are sure that both thesis and antithesis can be defended.)
5. Give at least one reason (or one piece of evidence) supporting your antithesis.
6. Give at least two reasons (or pieces of evidence) supporting your thesis.
7. Write a paragraph based on your thesis. Include in this paragraph the point supporting the antithesis and both the points supporting your thesis. Bear in mind that your purpose is to persuade a reader to agree with your thesis. Organize your paragraph in the way that seems to be best for this purpose.

VOCABULARY

1. Find a synonym (word or phrase) to use in place of each of the italicized words in the sentences below. Rewrite the sentences if necessary.

   a. Everything he had to say on the subject was the *antithesis* of all I believed.
   b. *Urban* areas were hardest hit by the power shortage.
   c. That point is not *arguable*.
   d. No *valid* reason exists for saying a thing like that.
   e. Can you *formulate* a good thesis on a subject relating to the environment?

37

2. The words *principle* and *principal* are often confused because they sound alike although they are spelled differently and have different meanings. Sometimes the only way to master such words is to invent some private trick—a rhyme, a joke, any kind of nonsense that will help you remember their difference. It doesn't matter how silly it seems if it works. One student, for example, wrote "I can remember that *principle* means 'rule' because it ends like *disciple*, which reminds me of the Golden Rule." It worked for that student. What works for you? If you don't already have a trick of your own, make one up.

3

The Full and Final Thesis

In learning how to arrive at a thesis, you have already taken the first major step in improving your skill in writing essays. The next step is the preparation of a full thesis statement. This step may seem purely mechanical, and in a sense it is mechanical. You could learn to do it without ever knowing the processes it represents, just as you can turn an ignition key and start a motor without any understanding of the internal-combustion engine. Actually, your thesis is a kind of ignition key to your essay; until you turn it, your writing will generate no power.

But beyond this point the analogy breaks down. Ideas and engines are very different things. You can drive a thousand miles without understanding the principles of internal combustion, but you will not take a very long or very interesting trip in an essay unless you understand not only how to prepare a full thesis but why you do it. That *why* is very important.

First, however, you need to know exactly what is meant by full thesis.

Elements of a Full Thesis

So far, your thesis is simply your opinion sharpened to one pointed statement. Your *full thesis* will have three elements: (1) the thesis statement itself, (2) points that can be made against your thesis, and (3) points that can be made in favor of your thesis. Putting these three elements together in a full thesis statement requires no particular writing skill; at this point you are not concerned with stylistic flourishes. You are merely arranging, in an orderly way, the raw materials you will be working with when you write. The full thesis statement never appears in its original form in the finished essay. Nevertheless, its preparation before you start to write is supremely important, for it will serve as your one sure guide through the territory that lies ahead: the territory of argument.

The Psychology of Argument

The three elements of a full thesis represent the psychology of all argument, whether written or oral. The goal in any argument is identical to the goal in any essay—to win others to a particular point of view, to *persuade*. And the same three elements are always present in a successful argument, whether it is a written essay, a formal debate, or a family quarrel.

Suppose yourself in the midst of a typical family crisis. You want to borrow the family car to go to a party on the other side of town. The last time you drove the car, however, you dented a fender—a circumstance that causes your father to view any further driving on your part with something less than sympathy. How do you persuade him to let you use the car again?

If you are a person of few words and very little wisdom, you stride up to him, announce without preamble that you want the car, and wait to see what happens. Your father, if he is typical, will probably ask you if you have lost your mind. He may even shout a little, and wave his arms, and turn slightly purple.

Result: You don't get the car.

If you are a person of much emotion and little reason, you may use pressure tactics: "Gee whiz, Dad, I'm not ten years old. Other kids my age drive all the time. I dent one crummy fender and you act like I committed a crime. Good grief, you ought to know I didn't do it on purpose. Anyway, it seems to me like you'd want to do something nice for me once in a while. . . ." And so forth.

Sounds pretty adolescent, doesn't it? As certainly it is. Sincere, yes. Reasonable, no. It is simply a great incoherent jumble of injured emotionalism, and it will convince no parent that you are a mature and responsible person.

Result: You don't get the car.

So, if you are wise, you use a third approach. First of all, you modify that belligerent "I want the car!" It becomes a request rather than a demand: "I hope you'll consider letting me use the car tonight, Dad." Thus you recognize, by a process very similar to the process of qualifying a thesis, that the matter must be settled not merely on the basis of your private desires but on the basis of your father's authority. And your father, if he is a reasonable man, will be willing to hear you out. You are not groveling, but you are showing respect for his rights. And he appreciates it.

Then you admit that your father has good reason to mistrust your driving skill: "Dad, I know I was to blame for denting that fender last week." Your father is agreeably impressed by the good sense of this remark. He is willing to go on listening. Nothing softens the opposition so much as a graceful admission that it has some points in its favor.

And so you wind up your case with the arguments most likely to work in your favor: "But you see, I accepted the invitation to the party before I damaged the fender. Incidentally, I've already made arrangements to have it repaired. I'll pay for the damage myself. And I'd like another chance to prove to you that you can trust me to drive."

Result: You *may* get the car.

Your father, if he is a reasonable man, will at least be willing to consider your request fairly. And that is all, really, that you have the right to expect. But you have earned that right because you have presented your case as one reasonable person to another. You have not made a belligerent, unexplained demand ("I want the car!"), nor have you poured out an incoherent jumble of emotionalism ("I'm not ten years old . . . other kids . . . crummy fender . . ." and so forth). You have used, whether you know it or not, the psychology of argument. And it has a very definite pattern— a pattern identical to the one you will use in preparing a full thesis statement:

1. thesis (accurate, qualified statement of main idea): "I hope you'll consider . . ."

2. point that can be made against thesis: "I know I was to blame . . ."

3. points in favor of thesis: "I accepted the invitation . . . before . . . ," "I'll pay for the damage . . . ," "I'd like another chance to prove . . . you can trust me . . ."

Strongest Argument Last

Observe that even in the arrangement of your reasons you follow a pattern. The reasons are presented in an ascending scale, with the strongest (from your father's point of view) coming last. The fact that you accepted the invitation before you damaged the fender is relatively unimportant to him; the fact that you have taken responsibility for the damage is much more important—he begins to feel some respect for you at this point; but most important of all to him is your desire to prove your trustworthiness, for it appeals both to his sense of fair play and to his instincts as a father. You need only to reverse the order of your reasons to see how your case would be weakened in your father's eyes.

Every successful argument, written or oral, conforms to the pattern: statement of case, recognition of opposition, and defense, with the strongest argument placed last. All this may make an essay seem no different from a debate or a trial by law. As a matter of fact, the underlying logic is identical. The difference is simply in emphasis, in language, and in style of execution. A persuasive essay may seem as light as thistledown, as intimate as a friendly conversation, but always at its core is the same inescapable iron logic of argument. The pattern may be beautifully disguised, but it will be there.

Form of the Full Thesis

Type or write your full thesis on a card or a sheet of paper. Put it on the wall in front of your work place if possible; you should keep it in full view all the time you are working on your essay. The form is very simple. State your thesis and arrange your pro and con arguments below it. Your thesis on soccer, for example, would look like this:

Thesis: Soccer appears destined to surpass football in popularity in the United States.

CON—POINTS CONCEDED TO FOOTBALL	PRO—POINTS SUPPORTING THESIS
Football got there first; may be hard to dislodge	Costs less to equip team
Football may be a fan habit that's hard to break	Fewer serious injuries
Millions of dollars invested in football	Physical size less important
More openings for players on team	Good game for both sexes
Opportunities for specialists in football	All players take part in advancing ball
Claim made that violence of football is harmless outlet for potential violence of society	Action continuous; no long waits between plays; no long time-outs
	Chance for best players to compete internationally

This is your full and final thesis. A friend who may be convinced that football will never yield its popularity to soccer would make a similar listing, with some differences. The minor advantages that you concede to football become in your friend's full and final thesis the mainstays of the argument for football. With reasonableness equal to your own, your friend will concede to soccer any advantages that cannot be fairly and intelligently argued.

Thesis: Football must inevitably win any long-term popularity contest with soccer in the United States.

CON—POINTS CONCEDED TO SOCCER	PRO—POINTS SUPPORTING THESIS
It costs less to field a soccer team.	Money that football brings in more than makes up for the high cost of fielding a team.
Action in soccer is continuous.	With its numerous offensive and defensive maneuvers, football is sports action at its most varied.
Soccer places less emphasis upon the physical size of players.	Trend toward specialization has opened the game to the smaller player.
Each year, the number of Americans playing soccer increases.	In spite of efforts of promoters to popularize soccer, football fans have thus far remained loyal to their sport.

Here, in a nutshell, is the substance of an entire essay for either thesis. The con arguments are placed on the left for convenience as you write—you take care of these first. Then you can move on, developing fully the pro arguments that support your thesis.

Once you have this full thesis statement before you, a glance at it will tell you exactly what points you are going to make. Under con will be the points that can be made against your thesis; these you must be prepared to concede or to counter with reasonable argument.

Concession:
　　Admittedly football has the advantage of familiarity, but . . .

Counterargument:
　　Every day travel and television are introducing soccer to more and more Americans who . . .

Think of your con list as the points you will *concede* and of your pro list as the points you will *propound,* and you will be on safe ground. Your pro list will always be the longer one, of course, for this is the main body of your argument.

Your paragraphs will not necessarily follow the exact order of the points listed in your full thesis. The points are there to *guide* you, not to dictate to you. As you write, you may find that their position in the essay needs to be shifted. A point that seemed minor may suddenly assume a new importance; one that at first seemed major may dwindle to relative insignificance. But all your carefully-thought-out ideas are there, ready for you to develop.

What if your thoughts suddenly branch out, expand, bring new ideas that seem important? By all means take advantage of their possibilities. Never let a good idea get away from you just because you didn't think of it before you wrote your full thesis statement. But always check out each new idea. Ask yourself: "Is it related to my main point? Does it make my point clearer or merely confuse it? Am I putting it where it belongs, or would it be more effective in another paragraph?" If a new idea works, if it will help persuade your reader, then by all means use it. Never box yourself in so rigidly with a full thesis statement that you can't wander afield to make a related point.

The full statement will, however, prevent you from wandering completely off course. If you continually check your developing essay against it, you won't find yourself discussing soccer one minute and your pal Bill the next. You won't begin a paragraph on cheerleaders, bog down in a swamp of sentiment about misunderstood youth, and emerge ten sentences later with an observation on your Aunt Martha's chocolate pie. You will move freely around any point you wish to make, but you won't fly off in another direction altogether. Your full thesis is your check against the temptations of irrelevance.

The temptations are strong. If your ideas come thick and fast when you write, you are tempted to grab them all and stuff them into your essay willy-nilly for fear of missing one good point. If your ideas come slowly and painfully, you are tempted to use anything that occurs to you in the hope that it will somehow miraculously fit. The full thesis guards you against either of these extremes.

Summary

The full and final thesis of the general essay is the thesis plus a list of the points that can be made both for that thesis and against it. The list serves an extremely important purpose: When you finally get down to the actual job of writing, it provides a point-by-point chart of organization that will guide you through your entire essay. You should keep your full thesis statement on a card that is in full view all the time that you are writing. Use it not as a rigid outline but as a guide and a reminder. It will check your tendency to wander off course and will keep you constantly aware of the points you need to make.

The full thesis is a most remarkable and valuable device. Prepare it carefully, refer to it often, use it wisely. It will serve you well as you go more deeply into the structure of essays.

QUESTIONS

1. Define the full thesis of the general essay.
2. Explain the relationship of the full thesis to the psychology of argument.
3. Why should the full thesis statement be kept in view when you are writing an essay?
4. How strictly should you follow the full thesis when you write your essay?

ASSIGNMENT

1. Write a full thesis for each of the thesis statements below. Follow the form on page 43.

    a. The search for popularity generally leads to self-improvement.

b. The search for popularity can limit a student's personal growth.
c. Competition for grades is a healthy influence on students.
d. Competition for grades is an unhealthy influence on students.

2. Using your full thesis statement as a guide, write an essay of at least five paragraphs on one of the topics above. You must work into your essay *all* the material suggested by your full thesis. Develop and arrange your paragraphs in any way that seems effective, bearing in mind that your purpose is to persuade the reader to agree with your thesis. (Hold on to this assignment. You will use it later.)

VOCABULARY

1. Find a synonym for each of the following words:

adolescent	flourish (n.)	modify
analogy	groveling	preamble
belligerent	incoherent	propound
concede	irrelevance	relevance

2. Use each of the synonyms you have found for the listed words in a complete sentence. Each sentence must relate in some way to the problems of essay writing. Be as informal as you please—complain if you feel like it. But use the synonym, and be sure that your sentence bears some relation to essay writing. For example, you might write something like this, using *youthful* (the synonym for one of the words above):

It is a cruel and inhuman thing to curb my youthful spirit by forcing me to use logic in order to find a thesis.

4

Structure

The basic structure of the essay is extremely simple. It has three parts: (1) an introduction, (2) a body, and (3) a conclusion—or, to put it in even simpler terms, a beginning, a middle, and an end. If this strikes you as painfully obvious, you may be surprised to learn that failure to understand this simple arrangement probably explains the collapse of more essays than any other single factor.

If you are a beginning writer, it's likely that your tendency is to jump squarely into the middle of any essay you write, unloading everything you know about your subject as fast as possible, never mind in what order. Thus your essay will have neither a genuine introduction nor a genuine conclusion; all your information is piled into one big, disorderly, mid-section collection bin. You may have worked very hard to collect that information, but by the time you have it all put together in a single piece of writing, you begin to wonder whether it was worth the effort. Something is wrong with your essay, and you know it. But what? You feel almost as disconsolate and uncomprehending as the mad egg-lady who gathers her eggs with exquisite care, packs them delicately into her basket, and then weeps because they break when she dumps them on the floor.

Fortunately, as a writer you are not in quite so hopeless a situation as the egg-lady. If you scramble your basket of ideas the first time you try to unload them in writing, you can reassemble your collection and begin again. But you can save a great deal of time and wasted effort if you know in advance what you want to do with your ideas, realizing that when you write an essay you're confronted not with a dumping process but with a building process.

So think of yourself as a builder. And think of your essay as a *structure:* this basic structure is very simply illustrated in Figure 1.

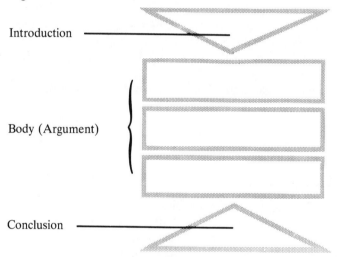

Introduction

Body (Argument)

Conclusion

Figure 1—Structure of the Essay

Think of each of the units in Figure 1 as one paragraph. Certain obvious characteristics show up at once: (1) The first, or introductory, paragraph begins broadly and narrows to a point. (2) The middle section, or argument, is in block form and takes up most of the space in the essay. (3) The last, or concluding, paragraph begins at a narrow point and ends broadly.

We will return again and again to this illustration as we progress, demonstrating methods of working with it, of tying the parts firmly together, of enriching it with detail. As it stands now, it represents the bare bones of structure, the steel framework upon which every essay must be built. *This basic structure never changes.* It may be so skillfully disguised by the author that you are not aware of its presence, but it is there. You will find it in every successful essay ever written, from the simplest to the most complex. It will differ only in details; the basic structure is always the same.

Just as different architects, beginning with the same basic design, will create completely different houses, so will essayists create different essays. Each will bring to every piece of writing a particular taste and style. What can be done to enhance the basic structure depends upon the individual writer's wit, imagination, vocabulary, and general ease with language. But no writer can escape the demands of structure in a standard essay.

So let's examine the three main parts of this structure and see how they work.

The Introduction

One paragraph is usually sufficient to introduce an essay. The structure of this paragraph is different from the structure of any other paragraph in the essay because its function is different. *The function of the introductory paragraph is simply to introduce the subject and come to the point.*

Figure 2—The Introduction

Examine this sample introduction:

> A sport almost without rival for the affections of European fans, soccer has had a hard time winning friends in the United States. Until recent years, Americans, caught up in their love affair with football American-style, had scarcely given soccer a second glance. But something has caused Americans to turn and look again. Suddenly the sport that had had trouble begging an invitation to an empty lot is now invited regularly onto some of the country's most exclusive playing fields. School teams and soccer leagues appear almost overnight. Summer camps where boys and girls learn the fine points of dribbling a soccer ball pop up on college campuses everywhere. Americans are succumbing to the appeal of Europe's version of football at an astonishing rate, with no end in sight. Soccer is finally winning its way in this country and appears destined to surpass football in popularity.

The paragraph, you will note, opens with a broad, general statement related to the thesis and then gradually narrows to a single point—the thesis itself. Sentence by sentence, it closes in on the thesis. Structurally it is a triangle resting on one point (Figure 2). It moves from the general to the specific, from "pan shot" to close-up, from broad observation to punch line.

That is its whole purpose—to introduce the subject in a general way and then come to the point. Here again you can see the psychology of argument in operation. Your thesis, remember, is an *opinion,* and nobody wants an opinion exploding in his or her face in the first sentence of a conversation, written or oral. (An essay, after all, is a kind of conversation between you and the reader.) So begin your introduction with a general statement and end it with your thesis statement.

Opening Statements

Understanding this structure is no problem for most students; the problem is in deciding just what kind of opening statement to make. What can you say that will be not merely a general statement but a general statement that will lead logically into a statement of thesis?

This depends largely upon how you plan to develop your thesis. (Thus you begin to reap immediately the benefits of all the work that went into developing a full thesis statement.) But as a rule of thumb, begin your thinking about an opening statement with one major element in your thesis (usually a noun) and make an observation about it that any sensible reader will find acceptable. In either of the two theses about soccer, for example, the following terms are the main elements:

soccer   football   United States   popularity

Or any of the terms below could be extracted by inference:

sport   sports fans   Americans   contest

In the example on page 51, *soccer* was used as the key word. But any of the other words extracted from the thesis, directly or by inference, could have served as well:

Football has become one of this country's major commercial enterprises.

We in the *United States* have not always been hospitable to European ideas, customs, or creations.

"Dancing," the late Vince Lombardi is reported to have said, "is a contact *sport. Football* is a collision *sport.*"

Sports fans tend to be creatures of habit.

Millions of *Americans* have grown up with the notion that on any Sunday afternoon between July and February, only one spot on Earth offers true comfort and joy: the chair closest to the television screen.

What could turn out to be one of the most fascinating *popularity contests* of the century is now under way.

Any of these opening sentences could lead to either thesis—the one favoring soccer or the one favoring football. The author has not yet taken a position. But the territory has been marked out and the subject to be covered generally announced. Moreover, the reader can sense that the writer plans to state a particular point of view by the end of the paragraph.

A kind of logic asserts itself as you work your way from the opening general statement to the specific thesis. You can see it easily in the example on page 51. The author has chosen to introduce the subject by means of a contrast: soccer loved in one place and largely ignored in another. But it is this contrast, this difference, that sets the general direction of the introduction. Whether the situation is going to change or is going to remain much the same will become clear as the paragraph moves along. But at this point the essay could have gone in quite the opposite direction just as well:

> A sport almost without rival for the affections of European fans, soccer has had a hard time winning friends in the United States. Its uphill struggle for support in this country is largely the result of a prior commitment millions of Americans have made to another sport: football. Although in recent years soccer has won numerous followers in the United States, its most ardent fans must recognize that it still trails hopelessly behind football in the popular fancy. They need only examine the sports pages of any daily newspaper to get the word. Football is king in the United States and is likely to remain so. In any long-term popularity contest with soccer in this country, football must inevitably win.

Other methods of opening with a general statement can be seen in the samples on page 52. Your choice depends upon the particular emphasis you want to give. But you can be guided by this general rule: Your opening statement will *relate* to your thesis but *will not take a position on it*. Then, by a process of qualifying, comparing, illustrating, and gradually limiting the subject, you quietly remove the major obstacles to discussion and get to the point. And there is your thesis at the end of the paragraph, clearly isolated and ready for examination.

Sometimes you may need to alter the wording of your thesis sentence in order to move into it smoothly and naturally. Change it if you must, but don't alter its meaning. Information, thought, and insight may cause your opinion to change, but verbal convenience should not.

No Bombs, Please

One of the commonest errors of beginning writers is to attempt a "terribly clever" opening. You should remember that the demand upon you is for clarity, logic, reasonableness—never for surprise or "gag lines." Your job is to convince the reader of the reasonableness of your thesis and thereby of your reasonableness and wisdom as a human being. Never try to be "cute." Almost without exception, the results are disastrous. Consider, for example, these typical "bombshell" openings:

> Wow! Just listen to those guys hit! Oomp! Bang! How those fans love it!

> Hey, come on! Let's go! This is Saturday p.m. knockin' on your door, and we've got a date with those bad Cats at the Stay-dee-um!

> Take fifty-thousand screaming citizens, a funny little checkered ball that goes "thooomp" and twenty-two guys in short pants running wild over the greensward, and you've got football English-style—soccer, that is!

Writing as painfully bad as this is born of a perfectly sound impulse—the desire to be interesting. Unfortunately, its effect is exactly the opposite. Almost invariably this kind of "sound effect" writing is merely a desperate attempt to cover up the absence of any real thought or imagination. It says nothing, but it makes a great racket. (The exclamation points alone are almost enough to cause permanent deafness.) The third example above is less noisy than very, very tired—the old "recipe-writing dodge" that was never very clever and has not improved with use. The road to interesting and colorful writing does not lie in this direction.

It lies, first of all, in an understanding of structure. The lamentable examples above would never have been written if their student authors had followed the simple structural pattern of the introductory paragraph: broad generalization narrowing to thesis. Remember, the function of the introductory paragraph is simply to introduce the subject and come to the point.

You will discover that it is usually necessary to rewrite your introduction after you have completed the middle section of your essay. Often this middle section opens up new ideas that you will want to incorporate in your introduction. But most writers find they simply cannot get into the main body of their essays until they have "primed the pump" with some kind of introduction, even though they must change it later. So the best policy is to get something down on paper, some general statement leading to your thesis, and then go back to it later, revising and rewriting as needed.

You may feel at first that the structural pattern of the opening paragraph is rigid and limiting, that it does not leave you free to be fully creative. It is, indeed, rigid and limiting—but that is the source of its strength. It provides a steel framework upon which you can build confidently. When you have mastered the basic structure, you can begin to experiment, to take artistic risks with your material. Far from boxing you in, the structure sets you free to create, to express fully the best that is in you.

QUESTIONS

1. What is the function of the introductory paragraph?
2. "The introductory paragraph can be described as a triangle resting on one point." Explain.
3. What is the psychological principle behind the practice of opening an introductory paragraph with a broad, non-controversial statement?
4. What is the rule of thumb for writing the first sentence of an introduction?
5. Why do beginning writers tend to use "bombshell" opening sentences? Why are such sentences nearly always failures?

6. The author suggests that mastery of structure makes it possible for you to express yourself more freely. Explain how this theory might be applied to one of the following activities: dancing, gymnastics, painting, automobile design, architecture.

Assignment

1. List the key words that come directly from the thesis of the essay you wrote for your last assignment (page 47).
2. Write an opening sentence for your introductory paragraph, using one of these key words. Remember that the sentence should be a broad general statement that does not take sides on your thesis.
3. Make a list of words or phrases that can be extracted by inference but that do not actually appear in your thesis.
4. Write another opening sentence for your introductory paragraph, using one of these related words or phrases. Model your sentence after one of the examples on page 52.
5. Rewrite your entire introductory paragraph. Use one of the opening sentences you have just written. Then close in on your thesis, following the form illustrated on page 51.

The Big Middle Section

The big middle section of your essay—everything between the introduction and the conclusion—can be almost any length.

Figure 3—The Middle Section

The number of paragraphs in it depends entirely upon how many points you want to cover and how thoroughly you want to cover them. It would be very foolish to decide in advance precisely how many paragraphs you intend to write—foolish and impossible. All sorts of influences begin working on you when you start writing. You will find yourself thinking, "I'd better use an example here . . . explain a little more clearly there . . . add this point . . . take that one out . . ." Almost the only rule you can follow is this: Write as much as you need to write in order to present your case clearly and completely and persuasively.

Whether your middle section is short or long, it is here that the real power of your essay resides. For the middle section is your *argument*. Here you put forward the reasons that will convince the reader of your thesis. And the most brilliant introduction will stagger in midflight like a faulty rocket unless you develop the middle section of your essay properly.

Midflight power depends upon many things, of course— vocabulary, tone, imagination, originality, style, all the skills of working with language. But the first consideration, the most crucial for the beginner, is *logical development*.

Refer to Your Full Thesis

Fortunately, you are already perfectly prepared. You took care of that when you worked out your pro and con arguments for your full thesis statement. There they are, lined up and waiting. Before you have finished writing, you may want to change the order in which you have listed them, but you needn't worry about that yet. Just get started, using your full thesis as a guide. You need only three general rules to guide you:

1. Make the necessary concessions to the opposition as soon as possible.

2. Devote at least one paragraph to every major pro argument in your full thesis statement.

3. Save your best argument for the last.

In a short essay, you can usually dispose of the opposition with one or two brief sentences. The whole purpose is to concede quickly the points that you do not want to dispute, or to set up quickly those that you feel must be disputed, and then get down to business—that is, to the presentation of your pro arguments only. So you waste no time. Immediately after your introduction, you make any necessary concessions:

Introduction:
> A sport almost without rival for the affections of European fans, soccer has had . . .

Thesis:
> Soccer . . . appears destined to surpass football in popularity.

First concession:
> *Admittedly, football now has the advantage of greater familiarity, of being a habit with millions. It has become a Sunday visitor in countless American homes.* But . . . [Paragraph goes on to point out that familiarity may be breeding contempt, that overexposure may be bringing on boredom, that boredom will cause a habit to crack quicker than anything.]

Second concession:
> *Hundreds of millions of dollars have been invested in football, amateur and professional. Investors expect their investments to pay dividends.* However, the sports dollar . . . [Paragraph develops the point that the sports dollar tends to follow fan interest. The clever investor will not lose, and so on.]

Note that these concessions take care of the first three con arguments listed under the full thesis in Chapter 3. Two of the concessions open paragraphs, but the paragraphs then move immediately into pro arguments that carry more weight than the concessions. You will probably do this naturally, but it's a good idea to keep the process consciously in mind. Never develop a con point as fully as you develop a pro point. Obviously if you give more space to your opposition than to your own point of view, you're likely to lose your readers to the enemy camp—or at least make them wonder whether you really believe in your own thesis. Worse, you may discover that you have chosen to defend the wrong thesis.

Notice that in the first concession above, you have actually disposed of two con arguments together. You can do this in a short essay if the two are closely related. In this case "familiarity" and "habit" are closely related.

Your decision on whether to present certain con points jointly or separately depends upon how much emphasis you want to give each point. If you want to give each point a paragraph, treat them separately. If they seem so closely related that one paragraph will suffice for both, treat them jointly. Never separate them and then repeat the same arguments just to fill up space. That never fools readers (or teachers). It simply bores and exasperates them beyond endurance.

In a very short essay, you may be able to dismiss all the opposition with a single concession. But if your thesis requires considerable explanation or a very involved defense, you may find it necessary to devote a full paragraph to explaining an opposition point. In that case you must follow it immediately with a full paragraph—or more—in defense of your own position. It's a simple matter of self-preservation. Never allow an opposing point of view to appear stronger than your own.

Whatever the length of the essay, the main idea is to get the opposition out of the way as soon as possible, both in the essay itself and in the individual paragraphs. For a clearer understanding of this structure, study Figures 4 and 5, on pages 60 and 61.

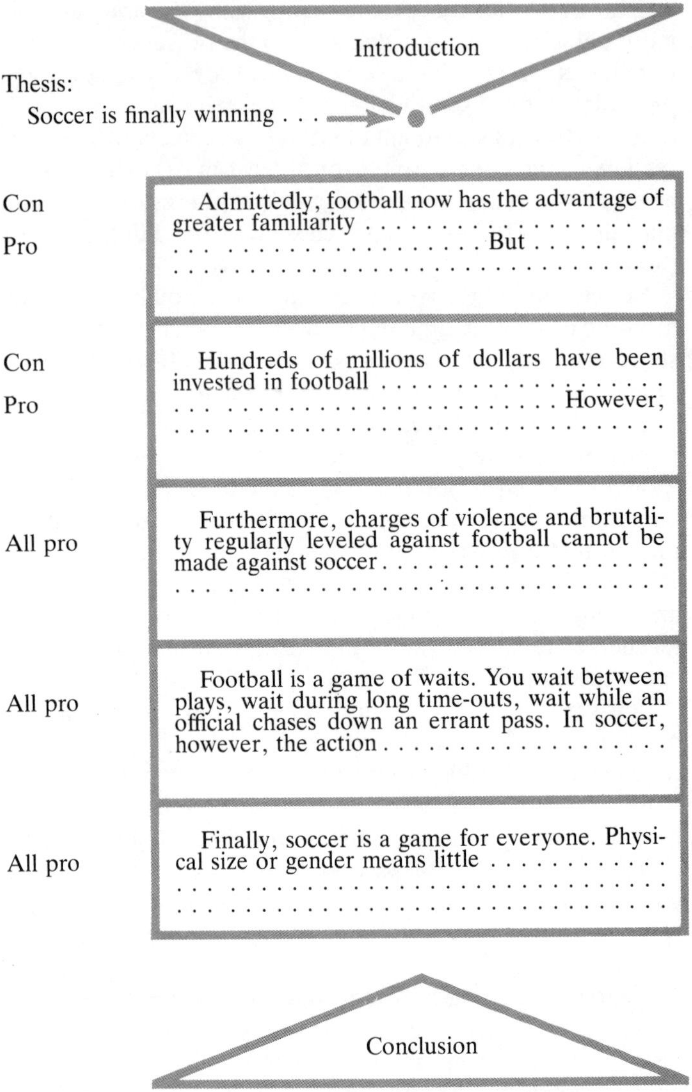

Introduction

Thesis:

Soccer is finally winning . . . ⟶

Con

Pro

Admittedly, football now has the advantage of greater familiarity . . . . But . . . .
. . . .

Con

Pro

Hundreds of millions of dollars have been invested in football . . . .
. . . . However,
. . . .

All pro

Furthermore, charges of violence and brutality regularly leveled against football cannot be made against soccer . . . .
. . . .

All pro

Football is a game of waits. You wait between plays, wait during long time-outs, wait while an official chases down an errant pass. In soccer, however, the action . . . .

All pro

Finally, soccer is a game for everyone. Physical size or gender means little . . . .
. . . .
. . . .

Conclusion

Figure 4—The Short Essay

60

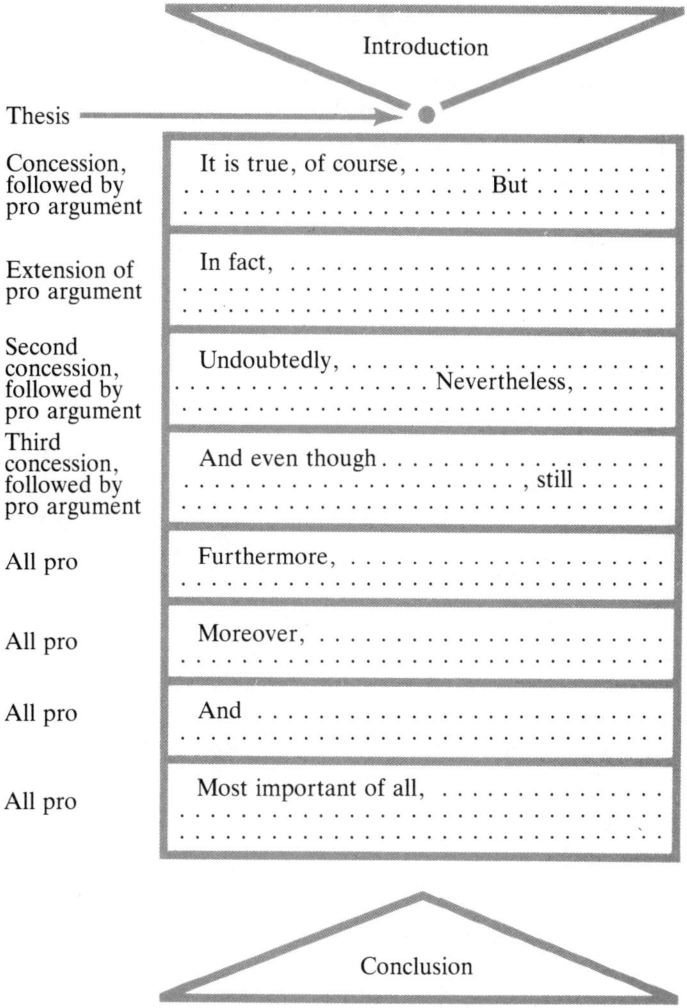

Figure 5—The Longer Essay

Bear in mind that the arrangement of early paragraphs here is suggested only. You may want to devote an entire paragraph to a concession or add extra "extensions" of pro arguments. But later paragraphs should concentrate on pro arguments only, as shown.

Note that the final paragraphs are devoted exclusively to pro arguments. It is always a mistake to allow reservations or concessions to crop up late; this weakens an essay disastrously. Your final paragraphs must be strong and assured, ringing with authority and conviction. Having vanquished your enemy, you need no longer concern yourself with further concessions. You have the floor, and you proceed confidently to take full advantage of it.

Your Strongest Argument

Remember that your final argument in this middle section should be your strongest. Naturally the question arises, "How do I tell which argument is strongest?"

The argument that *seems* strongest to you, the one that may have finally decided you in favor of your particular thesis, will probably be the strongest for your essay. But this is not always true—particularly if your emotions are involved. Remember that argument with your father over using the car? The strongest reason from your point of view was the invitation you had already accepted. But such an argument wouldn't cut much ice with your father—not after that dented fender. So you must be sure, in selecting your strongest argument, to base your choice not merely upon personal feeling but upon a sensible awareness of your reader's point of view.

Sometimes in the very process of writing, you will find the relative strength of an argument changing. Some point that seemed minor when you first wrote your full thesis may suddenly acquire new meaning and importance through a good example, a new insight, an unexpectedly effective use of words. Your own writing has convinced you that this minor point is not so minor after all; it may even strike you now as your real clincher. In that case, move it to last position. All your other arguments should then become stepping-stones to this major paragraph.

In short, *the middle section of your essay should always move toward its most telling paragraph.* Never commit yourself in advance to a rigid ordering of paragraphs. Your full thesis is a guide, remember, not a straitjacket. If your essay trades in humor, that last paragraph should be the funniest; if your essay emphasizes logic, the last paragraph should be the ultimate in logic; if your essay attempts to present an extremely complex idea, your paragraphs should move from the simplest possible presentation to whatever complexity is required to make your point. This is your last chance to convince your readers. Give them the best you have; this is where you clinch the argument.

QUESTIONS

1. "The real power of your essay resides in the middle section." Explain.
2. How does the full thesis help you in preparing the middle section?
3. Describe the method of handling opposition in both long and short essays.
4. What point should you make last in your argument? Why?

ASSIGNMENT

You have already written a new introductory paragraph for the essay assigned on page 47. Now, using one of the guides illustrated on pages 60–61, rewrite the middle section of your essay. Follow the guide as closely as possible. Remember, strongest argument last.

The Conclusion

You have introduced your subject, presented your thesis, and defended it. One step remains. You must wrap things up in one last paragraph and gracefully withdraw—you must write a conclusion. Otherwise, no matter how thoroughly you have explored every point in your full thesis, your essay will remain a piece of unfinished business, as unsatisfying as a piece of music that never hits its final note.

A student writer who has managed to put together with style and dash the greater part of an essay is often baffled by the attempt to conclude. Such a writer is like the guest who doesn't quite know how to go home, and who therefore stands irresolutely at the door, forcing the conversation to go on and on—and driving everybody within earshot mad (or putting them, finally, to sleep). Eventually, incapable of leaving gracefully, the guest makes a wild bolt for it—which, for the essayist, is the same as not writing a conclusion at all.

"But I haven't anything else to say," the student complains. "I've used up everything in my full thesis. Where do I look now for ideas?"

The answer may come as a surprise: Look in your introduction.

Back to Beginnings

You have come a long way from that opening paragraph. How can you make a connection at this late date with those distant sentences, written when your essay was only a few notes on a card?

Not only *can* you make a connection, but you *must* make it if the paragraphs you have written so far are ever to take on the solid shape and feel of an essay.

Since so much depends upon this connection, it makes sense to take a final, critical look at your introduction. Can you see any way to improve that first paragraph? In all likelihood, you can. The process of writing the middle section nearly always opens your eyes to new possibilities for your introduction. So double back. Now is the time to rewrite it if it needs rewriting. Any improvements you can make will almost certainly be reflected in your conclusion.

Then, with your introduction in its best possible shape, it is time to think about your conclusion.

Understand the Structure

Again, an understanding of basic structure can help you. The structure of the conclusion (Figure 6) is exactly the reverse of the structure underlying your introduction, which began with a broad general statement and narrowed to its point, or thesis. *Your conclusion begins with the thesis and widens gradually toward a final broad statement.*

Figure 6—The Conclusion

So, to get your conclusion started, simply repeat your thesis sentence, adding an appropriate word or phrase, if necessary, to tie it in properly with the paragraph that preceded it:

Thesis:

> Soccer is finally winning its way in this country and appears destined to surpass football in popularity.

Restated thesis:

> Clearly, soccer is finally winning its way in this country and appears destined to surpass football in popularity.

And the first sentence of your conclusion is already written for you. You need only lift it out of your introduction and drop it into place.

Often, however, this straight transfer of thesis seems flat and uninteresting. In that case, vary the wording. You can vary it in dozens of ways without changing the meaning. The following variations, for example, do the trick without repeating the exact words of the thesis:

> The reign of football is doomed, for soccer is destined to rule.

> Every year, soccer is winning friends, largely at the expense of football, and it is only a matter of time until soccer has a majority.

From this point you will begin to broaden toward your final sentence. As you do so, you can make a still stronger connection with your introduction by picking up any significant word or phrase in it and working it into your conclusion. Every time you do this, you create echoes in a reader's mind, touch a nerve of remembrance. When you create echoes in this way, readers never think consciously, "Oh, yes, that was mentioned earlier." They simply experience that particular sense of satisfaction and completion that comes to all of us when we feel that everything is falling into place, that things "fit."

Sometimes it is possible to conclude a very short essay by borrowing only from the introduction. Ordinarily, however, you need further ties with the middle section in order to give your conclusion substance.

Tying In the Middle Section

Many student essays run aground in the final paragraph because the writer attempts to summarize the points that have been made simply by listing them:

> In the preceding paragraphs it was shown that soccer is safer, more economical, and more enjoyable for everyone.

This listing of points, as though you are adding up a column of figures, is deadly. And insulting. None of us likes to be reminded in this heavy-handed way of something we have just finished reading.

Try, instead, to suggest, to leave in your reader's mind a series of pictures rather than a series of blunt and graceless declarations. Borrow meaning from your middle section, borrow a few key words; but don't be flatly repetitive, don't make lists. Say what you have already said, but say it sharply, quickly, and in different words. Look at the difference in the two samples below, both written for an essay that stressed soccer's advantages over football:

> Consequently, soccer is finally winning its way in this country and appears destined to surpass football in popularity. The preceding paragraphs have shown that

soccer is less dangerous and is cheaper than football and that it provides more and faster action. In addition, it appeals to the old as well as the young and to members of both sexes.

Every year soccer is winning more friends in this country, largely at the expense of football, and it appears to be only a matter of time until it has a majority. Young people who want to play and older people who must be content to watch are finding soccer irresistible. Rest assured, the owners and sponsors who hold the checkbooks will follow where these new fans lead. All signs carry a clear message: American football is an endangered species, and soccer has made it so.

The first example repeats the thesis and summarizes the points as if they were items on a laundry list. The second varies the wording of the thesis and disperses the points in two sentences with different but related constructions.

And the essay has reached its end. The conclusion, borrowing from everything that has gone before, summarizing without repeating exactly, has given the essay its final shape, has made it into a complete, compact, self-sustaining unit.

Borrow. Suggest. Transform. Pull out words and phrases and place them in a new setting. *Remind your reader.* Then move outward with a statement that relates your thesis to a broader background, so that it can be seen in a last long perspective.

Remember, your conclusion is your last word, your last chance to persuade your reader of the truth in your thesis. Take advantage of it.

Summary

Think of your essay as a structure, as something that you actually build according to a definite architectural pattern. You will find it far easier to say what you want to say when you have a sense of structure, for it imposes on your thoughts the discipline of logic, which in turn develops your ability to organize and to make relationships.

Every essay has three major parts: (1) an introduction that states the thesis and that can be seen structurally as a triangle resting on one point; (2) a middle section, structurally a large block, made up of several smaller blocks of argument; and (3) a conclusion, another triangle, resting on a broad-based generalization related to the rest of the essay. An essay will have this structure whether it is long or short, and you can learn specific techniques for writing each of the three major structural parts and relating them to one another.

Once you have mastered this structure, you are ready for the really exciting part of writing: the study of style. That begins in the next chapter. Most of the writing you have done so far has simply familiarized you with your instrument. Soon you will discover what kind of music it can make. But be sure you know your instrument first. Stay with structure until you understand it thoroughly.

QUESTIONS

1. Since the middle section of an essay covers all the points in the full thesis, why does an essay need a concluding paragraph?
2. How does the introduction help you write a conclusion?
3. Why is it likely that you will need to rewrite your introduction before writing a conclusion?
4. Describe the structure of a conclusion.
5. "Every time you pick up a significant word or phrase from preceding paragraphs and work it into your conclusion, you create echoes in a reader's mind." Explain this statement.
6. How can you summarize without listing?
7. Explain what is meant by "broadening" your concluding paragraph to its final sentence.

ASSIGNMENT

1. You have now rewritten all of your original essay. Carefully read everything you have written. See if you can

improve your introduction. Then write a conclusion, following the form on page 65.

2. Write a complete essay on a topic of your choice, following the structure outlined in this chapter. (Be sure to prepare a full thesis statement first.)

1. Using your dictionary, write a definition for each of the following words:

argument	intolerably
close-up	irresolutely
discipline	lamentable
disconsolate	pan shot

2. Each of the words above is used here in a complete sentence followed by part of another sentence. Finish each of the incomplete sentences so that it *explains or illustrates* the first sentence.

    a. Most people think of an argument as a quarrel. In an essay, however, an argument . . .

    b. She was disconsolate. She . . .

    c. The man was intolerably rude. He . . .

    d. The boy stood irresolutely at the door. He could not decide whether to . . .

    e. Her wardrobe was in lamentable condition. Everything she owned . . .

    f. The close-up scenes were particularly effective. One shot concentrated on the old man's hands, and you could see . . .

    g. Films often open with a wide pan shot. In a western movie, for example, the camera usually sets the scene by . . .

    h. The discipline she imposed on herself was extraordinary. She never . . .

5

First Steps Toward Style

By now you should have the feel of an essay, the sense of it as a structure. Structure alone, however, does not guarantee a good essay any more certainly than an artist's first charcoal sketch on canvas guarantees a good oil painting. The original sketch may be strong, interesting, and full of promise, but the final judgment of the work rests upon the artist's use of paint.

In the same way, the final judgment of a piece of writing depends upon the writer's use of words.

You may have a brilliant thesis. You may have devised for it an impressive structure, unassailable in its logic and perfect in its proportions. And you will have thus proved that you can think and that you can organize—two skills essential to good writing. But now you are face to face with the actual job of *writing,* of choosing the words and shaping the sentences and developing the paragraphs that will say best, most clearly and effectively, exactly what you want to say.

You are, in short, up against the problem of *style.*

Style in writing is like style in anything else—some special quality that commands interest or gives pleasure, something that makes you sit up and take notice. It shows up in all sorts of places, and it's always easy to spot. At a basketball game, for example, you may find yourself watching one particular player most of the time. The player may not be the team's highest scorer but is such a pleasure to watch in action that you pay little attention to anybody else on the floor. Pressed to explain your obvious preference, you might say, "That player seems to do everything so easily."

That's style.

Style is perhaps best defined as this ability to do something difficult as though it were easy. Invariably we respond to it with delight. We may appreciate the points made for our team by the ball player who pants and stumbles and strains for every shot, but the player who gets our praise is the one whose every move seems effortless.

The principle is the same in writing. You are bored by the writer who makes every point laboriously, painfully, in dull and awkward language. Yet a writer who makes exactly the same points without apparent effort, in language that seems as easy to understand as good conversation, will hold your interest.

This air of effortlessness, whether in ball playing or writing (or, for that matter, in singing or ballet dancing or playing the tuba or juggling six oranges), is deceptive. For its secret is control. And control is a hard-won thing. Ball players don't have that perfect hook shot handed to them on a platter by Mother Nature. They *learned* it—and they learned it through hours of patient, disciplined practice in an empty gym. Writers, you may be sure, are not born knowing how to put words together to best effect. They *learn* this skill, and they learn it in the same way ball players learn theirs—through self-discipline and practice.

Style, in other words, is not a mysterious gift reserved for the lucky few. It is something you learn. You may feel that you have no talent for writing, no special gift. And you may be entirely correct in this assessment of your abilities. "Nobody," you may say, "can learn to be talented." Correct again. But you *can* learn style. For style is not a gift. It is technique. It is the "how" of writing as opposed to the "what." No matter what you have to say, you can learn to say it well. And that is style.

It takes practice. You must perfect your ability to handle language through hard work at the typewriter or with paper and pencil. This means learning not only what to do but what *not* to do.

And that is the place to begin.

You are about to be presented with two rules that may strike you as peculiar or simply maddening. Or downright irrelevant. Peculiar they certainly are, for you will learn them for only one reason: so that you can break them intelligently when you are more experienced. And maddening they may well be, for they may cut you off from the only kind of writing that makes you feel secure. But irrelevant they are not. They will teach you quickly some things about style in writing that would take years to learn through trial and error.

Bear in mind that these rules are temporary. When you have practiced them long enough to make them part of your working equipment, you can break them with the assurance that comes from knowing exactly what you are doing. But for the present, until and unless you are otherwise instructed, they are to be your Two Commandments:

1. Do not use first person.
2. Do not use the word *there*—ever.

The First Commandment

In most of the essays or themes that you have written in the past, you have probably made liberal use of the first-person pronoun. Youthful efforts at self-expression are nearly always thick with "I think . . . ," "I believe . . . ," "I feel that . . . ," "It is my opinion . . ." The habit of using the first-person pronoun to express an opinion is, in fact, so ingrained in some students that they honestly believe it is impossible to express an opinion without using the word *I*.

They are mistaken. The truth is that an opinion is almost always more forceful and convincing if it is presented without the first-person pronoun. In the following pairs, which statements carry more conviction?

> I believe that God exists.
> God exists.
> It is my opinion that smoking causes cancer.
> Smoking causes cancer.

Obviously the second statement of each pair carries far more punch than the first—*and it says exactly the same thing.* It merely says it more briefly, more forcefully, with a greater air of authority. Whenever a phrase containing a first-person pronoun is attached to an opinion, the opinion immediately becomes weak and defensive. It sounds vaguely apologetic. That nervous "I think . . ." seems to imply, "What I think isn't very important, but anyway I think that . . ."

The fact is, of course, that the student who feels compelled to attach a personal pronoun to every thought is not really writing about the subject at all. That first-person pronoun pushes the writer between the reader and the subject— usually to the reader's great annoyance. Notice, in the examples following, how surgery on the first-person pronouns forces the real subject to the fore:

> I think a good way to handle this matter is by student-body vote. I don't see how anybody could object to that.
>
> A good way to handle this matter is by student-body vote. Nobody could object to that.
>
> To me, Mark Twain's writing is very funny, but I think it is also very bitter.
>
> Mark Twain's writing is very funny and very bitter.
>
> I never know what to think when people behave like that.
>
> Such behavior is always puzzling.

It is helpful to remember that *I think* and *I feel* and similar expressions are actually redundant; they aren't needed, and they get in the reader's way. As the writer, you are always lurking in the background of your essay. Your reader knows

73

this, knows that every opinion you express is yours unless you state otherwise, so why add an *I think* to it? Obviously you think it or you wouldn't say it.

But don't try to conceal an *I think* or a *My opinion is* by converting it to a phrase like "The writer thinks" or "In the opinion of the writer." This is merely substitute first person; it replaces the first-person pronoun with an even more annoying obstacle to the reader's wish to get at the meaning of a sentence. The personal pronoun, instead of disappearing entirely, merely hides itself under a layer of cotton wool. Sentences like this develop:

> In the opinion of the writer, something should be done about the problem immediately.

> The position of the author is that eventually we will all pay.

Notice how much crisper, how much more direct and authoritative, the sentences become after surgery:

> Something should be done about the problem immediately.

> Eventually, we will all pay.

The urge to use first person is so powerful that few students can give it up without a struggle. Many try to take refuge in the impersonal *one* ("One never knows what might happen.") or the second-person *you* ("You can't help liking this book.") or, as a last sad resort, a substitute second person ("A person should always have a good study plan."). Surgery will not work for these. If you cut them out entirely, the rest of the sentence won't make sense. So the thought must be rephrased, using third person:

Impersonal to third person:
> One never knows what might happen.
> Anything might happen.

Second person to third person:
> You can't help liking this book.
> This book is irresistible.

Substitute second person to third person:

> A person should always have a good study plan.
> A good study plan is essential.

Notice that in each case the sentence becomes not only more direct and vigorous but also *shorter*. Yet its meaning remains exactly the same. All the words that contribute nothing to meaning or style have simply been cut out. And that is one reason for restricting yourself, for the present, to writing in third person. It offers valuable training in the art of saying what you mean, directly and forcefully.

This is not to say that you should never use first or second person. Some of the finest essays in the language have been written in first person. And this textbook makes liberal use of second person because it tends to personalize instructional materials. But you must earn your right to use these other modes of address. And you earn it by learning first of all to speak with authority and assurance in third person.

So train yourself to write, for the time being, in third person only. It is a habit that offers many unexpected rewards. You will find yourself thinking clearly rather than feeling vaguely. You will concentrate on your subject with greater intensity, thus discovering not only more things to say but more direct and vigorous ways of saying them. Above all, you will be more logical—and, for the essayist, logic is the basic weapon. Third person forces you to be logical, for it requires you to throw away the crutch of the first-person pronoun and to consider your arguments with the same kind of coolness and detachment that you can expect from your reader.

Mastery of third person will give you a powerful new sense of authority and control. Gradually this new sense will make itself felt in everything you write. When you finally return to first person, you will be able to use it far more effectively than ever before.

The full command of third person is not something you are likely to achieve overnight. Your first attempts at it, in fact, may be accompanied by howls of frustration. But with practice you will discover its enormous range and flexibility, its potential not only for brisk and forceful statement but for graceful expression.

So practice it. In the assignment at the end of this chapter, and in all the assignments for the next several chapters, you will be asked to use only third person. You have been using first and second person, and awkward substitutes for first and second person, as crutches. Now you must put your crutches aside and learn to walk alone.

Don't worry if you stumble a bit at first. Eventually you'll find your balance.

The Second Commandment

Don't use the word *there*.

An easy rule to follow? Don't be too sure. If you are like most people, you probably haven't the faintest notion of how often you use this harmless-looking little five-letter word. Stopping its use may be almost as hard as stopping a nervous habit like doodling or eraser-nibbling. You don't even know you're doing it until somebody points it out to you.

The trouble with *there* has nothing to do with grammar or with "correctness" of any kind. It's a perfectly proper word, and it moves in the best circles; you will find it in abundance in the work of the most distinguished writers. But the fact remains that it is one of the most insidious enemies a beginning writer faces in the search for style.

It is the enemy of style because it seldom adds anything but clutter to a sentence. And nothing saps the vitality of language as quickly as meaningless clutter. Look at this sentence:

> There was something wrong.

Now look at the same sentence without the *there*.

> Something was wrong.

The greater urgency of the second sentence should be obvious; of the two, it's the one more likely to convince you that something is *really* wrong. As a reader, you are alerted by that direct, straight-to-the-heart-of-the-matter statement. Clutter it up with *there was* and all the strength oozes out of the sentence.

Sometimes you need only cross out *there* and juggle the words slightly to create a better, more direct sentence. But this won't always work. What would you do, for example, with a sentence like this?

> There was a fight.

If you cross out the word *there,* you won't have the right words to make a sentence. Even after juggling, the best you can come up with is this:

> A fight was.

And that doesn't make sense. (To see how silly it can look, try it in context with one or two other sentences: "The crowd grew bigger. A fight was. The police had to be called.")

Obviously, the trouble is not merely with *there* but with the two words *there was.* Remove both of them, and you are left with the one important element in the sentence—a fight. Ask yourself what verb would work with it, and your problem is solved:

> A fight *broke out.*
> A fight *developed.*
> A fight *erupted.*

Any one of these or several others (*began, started, ensued, threatened*) would do the job—although *erupted* is probably the best because it is the most graphic. The point is that any appropriate active verb will give your sentence more life and vigor than the flabby and colorless *there was* construction.

Frequently a sentence containing this construction will end in a prepositional phrase:

> Somewhere there was the creaking sound of a door.

Again, by taking out the *there was,* you are left with something that is not a sentence. But you can make it into a sentence with remarkable ease by moving the object of the preposition so that it becomes the subject:

> Somewhere a door . . .

Add a verb and you will have a sentence that says in four words what it took nine words to say when you used *there was:*

> Somewhere a door *creaked.*

You could have written, of course, "Somewhere a door made a creaking sound." But that is a waste of words—you are using four words (*made a creaking sound*) to say what could be said more crisply with one (*creaked*). One characteristic of good style is the ability to pack as much meaning as possible, without loss of clarity, into as few words as possible.

> Then there was a speech by Henry.
> Then Henry spoke.
>
> Suddenly there was the sound of a motor.
> Suddenly a motor roared into life.
>
> At midnight there was a break in the dam.
> At midnight the dam burst.

Rip out *there was* and immediately Henry's speech is a little more important, the sound of the motor a little louder, the breaking of the dam somehow more disastrous. Why? Because each statement has become sharper, more direct, through the removal of meaningless words and the addition of "soundtrack" or "motion-picture" verbs: *spoke, roared, burst.*

Never underestimate the power of verbs that *show* what they mean. And never underestimate the weakness of a pure verb *(is, was, are, were, have been, had been,* and so on), particularly when it is attached to the word *there.* Pure verbs are simply verbs of *being;* they indicate existence and nothing else—no motion, no color, no sound. They turn sentences into mere snapshots of arrested movement, mere echoes of sound: "There was thunder and lightning." Active verbs are verbs of *doing;* they turn sentences into motion pictures with sound and color: "Thunder *crashed"* (or *roared* or *grumbled* or *muttered*), "Lightning *flashed* across the sky" (or *streaked* or *sliced* or *split* or *stitched* or *zigzagged*).

Our language is rich with motion-picture and soundtrack verbs; they are available by the thousand, ready to carry any shade of meaning. Yet the sad truth is that we make far too little use of them. With all these riches in the bank, we continue to write like paupers. And the *there*-plus-pure-verb habit is largely responsible. Only after you have conquered the habit will you begin to draw on the wealth of verbs that can give your writing life and strength.

Sometimes, of course, a *there* is really needed, as in the sentence, "I was there" (meaning literally, "I was in that place"). The word *there* used in this strict sense, is probably the clearest and simplest way to express your meaning.

Nevertheless, for the time being you must avoid even this use. It's too easy to confuse a necessary *there* with a merely convenient *there.* So avoid the word entirely. Kick it out of your vocabulary. Banish it. Send it to Siberia. As far as you are concerned, the word *there,* is poison, and *you are not to use it at all.*

That won't be easy. *There* is such a small word, so modest and well-behaved and familiar, that you literally no longer see it. You must learn to scan your written work with a cold, objective eye for every hidden *there,* to yank it out along with its lackluster verb, and to shape new sentences from the remains of the old.

This shaping of new sentences will lead you to new discoveries about language—its richness, its flexibility, its possibilities. You will learn what it means to *play* with language—to experiment, to juggle words into new patterns, to pick up sentences by their tails and turn them around, to pick and choose from a new wealth of verbs.

And when you have learned to do this, you will have come a long way toward style.

Summary

The Two Commandments represent way stations on the road to style. You have not yet finished with structure, but from this point forward, structure and style begin to merge. So you need to arm yourself now with the Two Commandments; they can give you immeasurable help in the writing that lies ahead. Get rid of *there*. Get rid of first person. Learn to do without them now in your writing, and when they are returned to you, you will be able to handle them with grace and skill.

The exercises that follow will help you establish the habit of writing without using the word *there*. Be prepared for some pleasant surprises. You will see an immense improvement in your work almost immediately.

QUESTIONS

1. In what way is style in writing similar to style in any kind of activity?
2. Why is it important to learn what *not* to do in writing? Give an example of the value of this rule in some other field such as golfing, bowling, swimming, acting, or singing.
3. Name the two rules that you are to observe in your writing until further notice.
4. Why does the use of the first-person pronoun frequently weaken a writer's statement? To support your answer, give examples other than those used in the text.
5. What is meant by the terms "substitute first person" and "substitute second person"?
6. How does the elimination of the word *there* from your written work force you to use better verbs?

ASSIGNMENT

1. Complete the sentences below so that they express your personal opinion.

    a. I think that student clubs . . .
    b. In my opinion, art classes . . .

    c. To me, the best movies . . .
    d. I feel that a college education . . .
    e. It is my belief that the color of a person's skin . . .
    f. One must pay close attention to most scientific lectures if . . .
    g. If you analyze television programming, you discover that . . .
    h. I don't see the point in requiring a person to . . .
    i. I feel almost certain that space travel . . .
    j. Nobody can convince me that . . .

2. Rewrite each one of your sentences in strict third person, avoiding all use of *I, me, my, one, you, a person,* and so forth.

3. Delete the word *there* from all the sentences below. Rewrite the sentences if necessary, using active verbs whenever possible.

    a. There is a girl in math class who has a brain like a computer.
    b. There are some aspects of this problem that can never be understood.
    c. Every member of the team was there when the coach made the announcement.
    d. There was the sound of running feet on the sidewalk.
    e. If there is one thing he can't stand, it's long telephone conversations.
    f. He was right, but there were moments when she hated him for it.
    g. There will be no meeting of the club tomorrow.
    h. There was a crowd of happy students in the hall.
    i. His point of view is strange, but there is a lot to be said in its favor.

VOCABULARY

1. Look up the definitions of the following adjectives:

| authoritative | objective |
| insidious | redundant |

2. In one sentence for each, explain exactly what the writer means in the sentences below. (Do not repeat the italicized word or any form of it.)

81

a. He could speak with an *authoritative* voice on the subject of space flight.
b. His political enemies tried to destroy him by *insidious* attacks on his loyalty.
c. They seemed utterly incapable of an *objective* point of view.
d. Don't make *redundant* comments.

6

The Size and Shape of Middle Paragraphs

Just as the structure of an introduction or a conclusion can be represented as a triangle, the structure of middle paragraphs can be represented graphically as rectangles, or blocks (Figure 7). It is helpful to think of these paragraphs quite literally as blocks—blocks of writing firmly separated from each other and making up the body of your essay.

You have been writing middle paragraphs all along, of course, with each essay assignment you have completed. But chances are you have never been entirely certain that your paragraphs succeeded—nor indeed that they were really paragraphs. What goes into a paragraph? How long should it be? How do you know where to start and when to stop? Exactly what *is* a paragraph? These are the questions that plague most students.

Occasionally you may be tempted to begin a new paragraph simply because you have the uneasy feeling that a particular block of writing is too long; you think the page will *look* better if you indent. So, willy-nilly, you indent, trusting to luck that the new arrangement is a paragraph.

Actually, such a principle is not all bad. The page *will* look better. An enormous, uninterrupted block of writing is a formidable thing on a page. It looks difficult and dull (and it usually is). The eye longs for variety, for pause, for some relief in the monotony of an unchanging typographical landscape. And that is one of the reasons for paragraphing: it makes the purely physical job of reading a great deal easier.

Figure 7—The Size and Shape of Middle Paragraphs

But that is only one of the reasons for paragraphing—and a minor one at that. If paragraphing involved no more than this, you could slice up long stretches of writing with a pair of scissors and call each slice a paragraph. Undoubtedly the new arrangement would look more interesting. Unfortunately, however, it wouldn't make much sense. Obviously, something a great deal more important than mere eye appeal is involved in paragraphing.

The important thing involved is, of course, ideas. The whole purpose of paragraphing is to separate ideas, to give each one its own setting so that it can be fully and clearly developed without interference from others.

Your first guide to this division-by-idea is your full thesis statement.

One Point, One Paragraph

Each of the major points you want to make in your essay is listed in your full thesis statement. Thus, if you have listed three points, you are automatically committed to at least three middle paragraphs.

But that's a bare minimum, hardly more than a starting point. For if your essay has any substance at all, each of your major points is likely to need considerably more discussion than a single paragraph can handle. In fact, it is very nearly impossible to state a major argument completely in one paragraph, precisely because it *is* a major argument. You will find yourself wanting to add an example here, to clear up a question there, to comment on related side issues. Thus, one major point may multiply into several paragraphs, each with its own small point to make.

Perhaps the easiest way to decide whether a minor point deserves a paragraph of its own is to think of your writing as talk. Each time that you would say, in conversation, "Oh, and by the way . . ." or "Listen, here's another thing . . . ," you would, in writing, start a new paragraph.

That's really just about all that paragraphing amounts to.

Length of Paragraphs

It is impossible to predetermine the exact length of any paragraph, just as it is impossible to predetermine the length of any essay. Too much depends upon what you want to say and how you want to say it.

You have often seen paragraphs that are very brief indeed—mere flashes of thought thrust between heavier blocks of writing. Sometimes a single sentence, even a single phrase, will have full paragraph indention.

Like this.

Such fragments, however, are not really paragraphs. They are rhetorical devices, attention-getters. They can be very effective, but their effectiveness depends mainly upon their contrast with the fully developed paragraphs around them.

You must therefore learn first the feel of a real paragraph—acquire a sense of what to put in, what to leave out, and where to stop. You can do this best by thinking in terms of big, fully developed paragraphs.

Try for a paragraph six or seven sentences long, with a total of about 125 words. That's a fairly substantial paragraph. By setting the length at this point, you force yourself to "think long," to exercise your imagination and ingenuity. Most students complain of being unable to find enough to fill out a paragraph; they express their main idea in one sentence and then go blank, unable to think of anything else to say. An understanding of paragraph structure will quickly solve this problem. In fact, you are likely to find it hard to keep paragraphs short enough after you understand their structure. But it is far easier to shrink a paragraph after it is written than to expand it. So try for the big paragraph.

Basic Paragraph Structure

The block structure of middle paragraphs (Figure 7), as opposed to the triangular structure of introductory and concluding paragraphs (Figures 2 and 6), should suggest immediately their major characteristic: they are solid, self-contained, fully developed units. Instead of moving toward or away from a point, each one *is* a point—a single point enlarged into a block of argument.

These blocks are, of course, related to each other, since each of them has the same basic purpose—to explain or illustrate some part of your thesis. Furthermore, they are linked together in various ways that you will study later. But in a very real sense, every paragraph is complete in itself. It can stand alone, with its own particular feeling of wholeness.

If you examine the block structure of a paragraph closely, you will discover that something rather interesting is going on inside it: the structural pattern of the essay is repeating itself.

Like the essay itself, every paragraph has three parts: a beginning, a middle, and an end. That's why it has a feeling of completeness. In effect, every paragraph is a miniature essay.

Nothing clears up the mystery of paragraphing so quickly

as this realization that a paragraph has three parts, a structure of its own. It has a *beginning,* called the topic sentence. It has a *middle,* consisting of several sentences that explain and illustrate the topic sentence. And it has an *ending,* called the concluding sentence.

The topic sentence, usually the first sentence of the paragraph, is simply an announcement of the particular point to be taken up in the paragraph. The point, of course, will be one of those you have listed in your full thesis statement, or a related subpoint. You need only write a complete sentence that sets this point forth clearly. That's your topic sentence. It tells your reader what the paragraph is *about.*

Follow this topic sentence with several sentences that explain and illustrate your point. That's your paragraph's middle section. And the very act of filling this out will drive you naturally toward a concluding sentence, a final flourish of words that seems to say "and that takes care of *that.*"

As soon as you begin to follow this three-part paragraph structure, you will discover that the "one point, one paragraph" rule will take care of itself. For if you introduce your paragraph with a topic sentence, devote the middle of the paragraph to explaining and illustrating the topic sentence, and then draw your conclusion, you can't miss. You will have, automatically, a one-point paragraph.

The topic sentence and concluding sentence offer few problems. It's those middle sentences that dismay most students. What comes between the topic sentence and the concluding sentence? How can you stick to the point without repeating yourself? How, in other words, do you develop a paragraph?

The answer is surprisingly simple.

Developing a Paragraph

Once you have stated your topic sentence, you do the most natural thing in the world: you explain and illustrate it.

You do this every day, unconsciously, in your conversation:

> "Man, I've never seen such a traffic jam. Cars were lined up all the way to Maxwell Bridge. Everybody was honking, and some guy in a blue Buick back of me was yelling like a madman—said he'd miss his plane and he'd sue the mayor or something . . . ."

> "It was hard work. Up every morning at five and out in the fields by six. Digging holes for fenceposts, running the tractor, hoeing corn—you should have seen the blisters on my hands the first week . . . ."

> "I'm scared to death of dentists. The minute I sit down in that chair, my knees turn to water and the old pulse goes up to about 180 . . . ."

These are just random bits of talk, the kind you use or overhear every day. The speaker might wind up with something like this:

> "Man, I've never seen such a traffic jam . . . .
> . . . .
> . . . . It was probably the biggest snafu in the history of the automobile."

> "It was hard work . . . .
> . . . .
> . . . . I never worked so hard in my whole life."

> "I'm scared to death of dentists . . . .
> . . . .
> . . . . One look at a dentist, and I turn into the world's biggest coward."

Observe the pattern. First the speaker makes it clear that the subject is something in particular: a traffic jam, hard work, fear of dentists. These are all clearly topic sentences.

Now notice what follows this topic sentence. The speaker illustrates it and gives specific details: a blue Buick and a yelling man; fenceposts and tractor-driving and blisters; knees turning to water. Then comes the final statement bringing the comment to a close. Listen carefully to the conversations that go on around you (or to your own), and you will see this pattern illustrated again and again.

People taking part in a conversation are usually quite unaware, of course, that they are following any kind of pattern. Questioned about it, they would probably respond with laughter. "Pattern? What a crazy idea. That's just the natural way to talk." Which, of course, it is.

It is also the natural way to write paragraphs. The pattern, or structure, is exactly the same. State your point. Explain or illustrate your point. Conclude. The pattern is identical whether you are talking or writing. You use the pattern every day in conversation without knowing you use it. Start using it consciously in your writing, and paragraphing will cease to be a mystery.

Your writing, of course, will have a different tone from your ordinary speech, for you aren't chattering with a friend when you write—you are putting yourself on record for people who read. Therefore, you will select your details with greater care and draw upon a richer vocabulary than you ordinarily use in conversation. Your tone will be informal but not careless and slangy—slang can often be effective in speech, but it usually sounds puerile in writing. Ideally, your tone should be informed, intelligent, and friendly.

The pattern is the same one you use in speech: topic sentence, explanation and illustration, conclusion.

Picture-Frame Paragraphs

The paragraph pattern will be very easy to master if you force yourself to *visualize* what you want to say in those middle sentences. Write your topic sentence; then ask yourself what kind of photograph you would take, or what kind of picture you would paint, to illustrate your point. Give yourself time to see this picture clearly in your own mind. Then put the picture into words, using detail as a photographer or a painter would use it.

The result will be a vivid picture framed between the topic sentence and the concluding sentence. Your reader will *see* what you mean. You are *showing,* not telling.

The practice of using specific illustrations and vivid detail, of showing rather than telling, is perhaps the most important difference between interesting and uninteresting writing:

> The children of the slums live in a world that few other children in America encounter. They live in terrible poverty. They do not have the advantages that other children accept as a matter of course.

You can read that without any real stir of interest. It tells but it does not show. Supply the reader with pictures, however, and interest goes up immediately:

> The slum child lives in a world that few other children in America ever encounter. Home is a cold-water flat, a place of peeling wallpaper and crumbling plaster and the ugly, scuttling sound of rats.

Notice that the word *poverty* does not even appear in the second example, yet unquestionably the *effect* of poverty is greater. You no longer have the vaguely general term "poverty." You have a *picture*. The writer is acting as both a motion-picture camera and a tape recorder, picking up actual, *specific* sights and sounds that add up to something far more convincing than any abstract word.

Notice also that the topic sentence has undergone a slight change, from *children of the slums* to *slum child*. The effect of this is to increase dramatic impact; the writer moves in, just as a motion-picture cameraman moves in, for a close-up shot. One deprived child, seen as an individual, is far more real and dramatic to the reader than any generalization about "children."

The more color, sound, and movement you can work into your middle sentences, the more convincing your picture will be. This is true even with essentially undramatic material. For example, one writer might describe a winter day like this:

> It was very cold. It was so cold that nobody wanted to stay outside. Everybody found this kind of weather very uncomfortable.

Another writer, with a better eye for detail, might put it this way:

> It was very cold, so cold that the atmosphere itself seemed almost solid. On the sidewalks, ridged and lumpy with caked ice, dirty crystals of old gray snow crunched underfoot with a dry, splintering sound. The trees were black skeletons, their bare branches crackling and snapping in the frigid air like an old man's bones. On the playground a deserted sled lay on its back like some great sprawled insect, its runners coated with ice. Even children stayed indoors on a day like this. It was too cold to play.

The first paragraph *tells* the reader; the second paragraph *shows*. It is hardly necessary to point out which is more effective.

In paragraphs that must carry some main line of argument, the picture-frame technique will vary somewhat. If your thesis, for example, is "Typing should be a required course," and your topic sentence is "The student should be required to type every paper handed in," you might have a paragraph like this:

> The student should be required to type every paper handed in, particularly for English classes. This would not only conserve the eyesight and sweeten the disposition of the teacher—it would help the student learn. No longer able to hide spelling errors behind blots and erasures and unrecognizable squiggles or simply to fatten essays with enlarged handwriting, the student will come up with some real ideas—properly spelled. Silly statements dashed off just to fill up space have a way of looking very silly indeed, even to their author, when they are neatly lined up in precise and impersonal black type. The student will view errors with a new and painful clarity, thus becoming both a better writer and a better student.

Note that in this case the topic sentence represents a clear line of argument ("The student should be required . . ."), and thus presents a somewhat different problem from the paragraphs on page 90 and on this page, in which the topic sentences are primarily statements of fact ("The slum child lives . . ." "It was very cold . . ."). An argumentative topic sentence requires more than pictorial detail; it must be supported by concrete examples to back up the "why" as well as the "what" of its statement.

That word *concrete* is important. *Concrete* means "real, specific, actual." To recognize the importance of concreteness, you need only see what would happen to the paragraph above if all the specific detail were removed:

> The student should be required to type all papers. This would make for easier grading. It would also lead to a general improvement in all the student's written work. . . .

The passage is not only less interesting but also less convincing. The two go together. If you want to interest a reader, use concrete examples full of specific details. In other words, don't just tell. *Show.*

Summary

The middle paragraphs of an essay constitute your body of argument, and the number of paragraphs you write for any essay depends upon the number of points you want to make. The length of these paragraphs can vary enormously, but for the time being, you should concentrate on writing fairly long paragraphs in order to get a firm sense of their structure: a beginning, a middle, and an end.

The easiest way to master this structure is by visualizing what you are writing about. *See* what you mean, then *show* your reader what you see, in a picture-frame paragraph—a paragraph in which the topic sentence and the concluding sentence act as a frame for a picture made vivid in your middle sentences with specific details.

Everything you write about will seem more real, both to you and to your reader, when you master the picture-frame technique. And you will find, as you move from point to point, explaining and illustrating as you go, that paragraphing has become a simple and quite natural process.

1. How does the structure of a middle paragraph differ from the structure of an introductory paragraph? from that of a concluding paragraph?
2. What is the main purpose of paragraphing?
3. Students of composition are advised to write "big" paragraphs while they are learning. Why?
4. In what way does the structure of a paragraph resemble the structure of a full essay?
5. What is the function of the first sentence in a paragraph? What is this sentence called?
6. What is the function of the middle section of a paragraph?
7. Why does the three-part paragraph structure automatically ensure the "one point, one paragraph" rule?
8. How does paragraph structure resemble conversation? In what way will it differ?
9. Explain the picture-frame paragraph. Is this different from basic paragraph structure, or is it simply another way of describing that structure?
10. The picture-frame paragraph that is primarily descriptive will differ somewhat from one that is argumentative. How?
11. Analyze the following paragraph. What major rule of paragraph structure does it violate?

> The old-fashioned American kitchen was the living center of the American home. That was where the family ate its meals, where children studied and women sewed and men read the newspaper, where every family crisis was settled. It was a big, warm, cluttered place, full of all the smells that meant home—freshly baked bread and starched curtains and stick cinnamon and scrubbed linoleum and apples and oilcloth. The kitchen was really the *living* room—the place where the family lived. The mothers in those days did not usually hold jobs outside the home. Children also learned to help with the chores around the house.

1. Write a paragraph (using correct paragraph structure) explaining what is wrong with the following paragraph. Be explicit.

> Too many students believe that popularity depends not upon what they are but upon what they have. They want their parents to buy them all the things that they feel will guarantee popularity. They feel that these things will solve all their problems and make them happy. This may affect their personalities in a very bad way.

2. Rewrite the above paragraph, using the picture-frame technique.
3. Write a paragraph that is primarily descriptive, beginning with this topic sentence: "The day was wet and rainy."

VOCABULARY

1. Write a definition for each of the following words:

graphic	puerile	willy-nilly
ingenuity	rhetorical	
predetermine	visualize	

2. Finish each of the unfinished sentences below so that it will demonstrate your understanding of the meaning of the italicized word.

   a. Her description of the thief was *graphic*. She made us see him as a . . . in . . . , with . . . and with . . .
   b. She had shown a great deal of *ingenuity* in making her.costume for the party. She had . . .
   c. You can't *predetermine* the length of any paragraph because, in the course of writing it, . . .
   d. Most of his attempts to prove his sophistication are *puerile*—for example, his habit of . . .
   e. Don't give me *rhetorical* answers. Give me an answer that tells me . . .

f. The boy had never been to the small town where his father had grown up, but he could *visualize* it. He thought of it as . . . (Use several details.)
g. It seemed to her that she had spent her entire life doing what other people told her to do, *willy-nilly*. She wished that, just once, she could . . .

7

Connections Between Paragraphs

In Chapter 6, you took a close look at the paragraph to see how it was made, examining it apart from the whole essay just as you might examine a carburetor apart from an engine or a single musical phrase apart from a whole composition. You found that the paragraph has a certain wholeness or independence of its own; it could stand alone and still make sense.

You must remember, however, that no matter how well a paragraph stands alone, it is always just one small part of a larger whole—the essay itself. And in order to do its part in the whole operation, it must connect smoothly with the parts around it. Like a loaded car on a moving freight train, it carries its own separate portion of cargo, but it must be firmly coupled to the car immediately ahead.

As a matter of fact, it might not be a bad idea to think of your essay as a moving train. Your introduction is the locomotive; it commands a clear view of the track, gives a warning toot to announce its departure, and supplies the power to set all the wheels in motion. The body of your essay is the string of paragraphs behind that locomotive, each one a freight car with its particular load of thought. And your conclusion, of course, is the caboose—the little car on the end, commanding a view of the country just passed through.

One thing this analogy should make clear is that all those separate cars, if they are to reach their destination, must be firmly hitched together. (If they aren't, you might wind up with a locomotive in Chicago, a string of freight cars scattered over the landscape all the way from Bangor to Tallahassee, and a caboose left sitting high and dry on a siding.) In exactly the same way, your essay can fall apart disastrously unless your paragraphs are firmly linked together.

Figure 8—Connections Between Paragraphs

A single example should make this abundantly clear. Below are two "unhitched" paragraphs from a typical student essay.

> The United States was not prepared for war when the Japanese attacked Pearl Harbor. Most people had known war was coming, but plans to get the naval and military forces ready for it were still mostly just plans. The U.S. had no real striking force yet.
> The Americans went on the attack the following summer. A Navy and Marine force attacked Guadalcanal Island and captured the airfield.

The two paragraphs seem to have no relation at all to each other. Bewildered, the reader looks for a connection. Could these two paragraphs possibly have come one after the other in the same essay? The answer is yes—had they been properly linked:

> *Badly prepared as they were, however,* the Americans went . . .

Begin the second paragraph like that, and the reader follows the train of thought without the slightest difficulty. *Badly prepared as they were, however,* cues the reader in. The Americans were not really prepared for global war, but they went on the offensive where they thought they could and must.

These links between paragraphs are called *transitions,* or *transitional devices.* They have one purpose: to help the reader follow a main line of thought. As the writer, you know exactly what you have in mind each time you make a shift in meaning. But you can't expect your reader to know: unable to read your mind or hear the tone of your voice or see the expression on your face, the reader can catch only the signals you send through words.

If you hope to be understood, you must provide that reader with a clear transition—a word or phrase that will link the paragraphs together. Transitions between paragraphs fall roughly into three categories: (1) standard devices, (2) paragraph hooks, and (3) combinations of both these types.

The standard devices are simple and obvious; they are specific words and phrases, and using them is hardly more than a matter of selection. The paragraph hooks are more sophisticated—and more fun. And when you have mastered the technique of the hook, the combinations will come easily and naturally. No one of the three is better than the others; they are all useful and necessary.

The wise writer will make use of all of them.

Standard Devices

Perhaps you have already noticed that certain words and phrases recur often in your writing as you develop a thesis. If you want to acknowledge a point that isn't debatable, you may write, "It is true that . . ." or "Admittedly, . . ." or "Obviously, . . ." or any one of several similar expressions. These are the con transitions, notifying the reader that you intend to concede a point. A few sentences later you will come back with a "Nevertheless, . . ." or "But . . ." that clearly signals your intention to present arguments in your favor.

Such words and phrases are among the standard transitional devices for leading your reader through an argument. They reveal, briefly and efficiently, that conflicting points of view are being presented; without them, as you saw in the example on page 97, the conflicting statements seem quite irrational. Here are a few more examples to illustrate the difficulties you can run into:

> Pets are fun.
> They require a lot of care.
>
> The project had value.
> It wasted time.
>
> He was a brilliant actor.
> He often performed miserably.

These paired statements simply don't make sense. Yet the same statements become perfectly clear when they are supplied with transitions:

> *True,* pets are fun.
> *Nevertheless,* they require a lot of care.
>
> *Admittedly,* the project had value.
> *But* it wasted time.
>
> He was, *to be sure,* a brilliant actor.
> *Yet* he often performed miserably.

These examples are, of course, oversimplified in order to emphasize the necessity for proper transition. If each sentence were a fully developed paragraph, the problem of transition would be the same.

You will be tempted to believe that because a connection between ideas is perfectly clear to you as a writer it is also perfectly clear to the reader. It isn't. The reader needs to be reminded constantly of exactly where you stand. So never omit the transition between paragraphs as you move back and forth between pro and con arguments.

Not all the mechanical transitions, of course, can be classified as strictly pro or con. The transition you use, and how you use it, will depend upon the purpose of the paragraph it introduces. You will use one kind of transition when you are shifting your point of view:

> Pets are fun.
> *Nevertheless*, they require a lot of care.

You will use another kind when you are simply adding another paragraph in the same vein:

> Pets are fun.
> *Furthermore*, their play is instructive.

Other transitional phrases are mainly for emphasis, whether pro or con.

> Some pets are, *in fact*, a menace to lawn and garden.
>
> Some pets are, *in fact*, the most marvelous company you could ask for.

The best guide to transitions is common sense—and a list like the following. It should give you a word or phrase that will introduce almost any paragraph of argument.

Admittedly	In addition	Of course
And	In fact	On the other hand
Assuredly	Indeed	Still
But	It is true that	The fact remains
Certainly	Moreover	Therefore
Clearly, then	Needless to say	Thus
Consequently	Nevertheless	To be sure
Even so	No doubt	True
Furthermore	Nobody denies	Undoubtedly
Granted	Obviously	Unquestionably

This is a fairly comprehensive list of standard transitional devices. It is not, however, a complete list. One very important transitional word has been left out—the word *however.*

However is such a splendid transition, so useful, so convenient, so downright indispensable—and so often misused—that it needs special treatment.

A *Note on* However

The problem with *however* has nothing to do with its meaning. As a transitional device it means exactly the same thing as *but.* But *however* doesn't always sound right. The problem arises from its position in the sentence.

A student writer will almost invariably give *however* first position in a sentence:

> *However,* good study habits can't be established overnight.

Told not to use first position, the same student will make a flying leap and deposit it at the end of the sentence:

> Good study habits can't be established overnight, *however.*

Nothing is wrong with either of these positions grammatically. But something is wrong with them rhythmically. The best position for *however* is nearly always inside a sentence, between commas:

> Good study habits, *however,* can't be established overnight.

In a compound sentence, it will usually appear inside the first clause:

> Good study habits, *however,* can't be established overnight, and the sooner students learn this the better.

In a complex sentence, it can come either inside the main clause or after the dependent clause, according to the emphasis you prefer:

> Good study habits, *however,* can't be established overnight, as many students learn to their sorrow.
>
> or

101

> As many students learn to their sorrow, *however,* good study habits can't be established overnight.

In any case, *however* works best if it is inside the sentence. Just exactly why this position is best is one of those stylistic mysteries that can't really be explained. It simply sounds better that way. And the importance of sound can't be dismissed, even in silent reading. A reader's inner ear is always cocked and listening, registering every rhythm and cadence of printed language whether that language is spoken aloud or not. And that inner ear likes to have *however* tucked discreetly inside a sentence, usually at one of the following points:

After the subject:

> Electricity, *however,* changed the lives of farmers.
>
> Driving on the beach, *however,* can be a risky business.

After the verb:

> They believed, *however,* that right was on their side.
>
> The bus broke down, *however,* before it reached the school.

After an introductory phrase:

> In many small ways, *however,* the situation had improved.
>
> After dinner, *however,* they had time to talk.

Note that in all these sentences *however* is protected on each side by a comma. This is the *only* correct punctuation for a tucked-in *however.* Remember that, and you won't make the mistake of trying to use *however* between two independent clauses—a common mistake in student writing:

> He was a handsome boy, *however,* he was not very interesting.

That doesn't really make sense, as you can see the moment you put in the two commas. So you move your *however* and say what you really mean—thus discovering that you need two separate sentences:

102

He was a handsome boy. He was not, *however,* very
interesting.

Occasionally you will find yourself with a *however* that
simply refuses to be tucked into a sentence comfortably. In
that case, change it to *but* and put it in first position:

> She wanted to apologize, to explain, to let him know
> that she was sorry. *But* she was afraid of him.

Try reading these two sentences aloud, using *however*
instead of *but.* You will discover that no matter where you
put the *however,* it will have a flat and stilted sound. In some
mysterious way the word *but* (which will work only in first
position) immediately gives the sentence a more human and
natural tone.

Nobody can prescribe precisely when to put *but* at the
head of a sentence or when to use, instead, a tucked-in
however. This is something you must decide on the basis of
your own preference. Try them both for size; test them
against your inner ear for tone. But don't use one of them
exclusively. For the sake of variety, use first one, then the
other.

Paragraph Hooks

Although *however* and the other transitional devices listed
earlier are indispensable in writing, making possible dozens
of neat and efficient connections, they can't handle the whole
transitional load. Even if they could, no writer would depend
upon them exclusively, for they can become painfully obvious when they are used over and over again. You want your
reader to be pleasantly aware that your paragraphs are firmly
linked. No reader, however, wants to see the chains too
clearly or to hear them clank too audibly into place.

So you need another kind of transition, something that is
both stronger and subtler. You have it in the *paragraph
hook.*

You probably use the paragraph hook often in your own
writing without knowing it and see it constantly in your

reading without realizing it (as in this sentence, for example). But to take full advantage of its possibilities, you should learn to use the paragraph hook consciously, to direct and control it for your own purposes. Control, remember, is the essence of style, and the handling of transitions is an important part of any writer's style.

To see how the paragraph hook differs from the standard transitional device, look first at the example below. Here the transition from one paragraph to the next is accomplished by a standard transition alone—the word *but:*

> Mark Twain is established in the minds of most Americans as a kindly humorist, a gentle and delightful "funny man." No doubt his photographs have helped promote this image. Everybody is familiar with the Twain face. He looks like every child's ideal grandfather, a dear old white-thatched gentleman who embodies the very spirit of loving-kindness.

Standard transition:

> *But* Twain wrote some of the most savage satire ever produced in America. . . .

The standard transition indicates clearly enough that the writer is preparing to take off with a new idea in opposition to the one in the first paragraph. But the transition is far too abrupt. The leap from one idea (how Twain looked) to the next (how he wrote) is simply too great to be handled by a mechanical transition. Observe how much more firmly the paragraphs hang together if the transition is made like this:

> . . . a dear old white-thatched gentleman who embodies the very spirit of loving-kindness.

Paragraph hook:

> The *loving-kindness* begins to look a little doubtful in view of some of his writing. For Twain wrote some of the most savage satire . . .

Here you see demonstrated the simplest kind of paragraph hook. The last word of the first paragraph is hooked into the first sentence of the second paragraph and used as a point of departure for introducing another idea. This repetition hooks the paragraphs together solidly. The hook need not be one word; it can be a phrase. It should not, however, exceed three or four words.

Although the last word or phrase of a paragraph frequently serves as the simplest and strongest kind of hook, you can go back farther than this, sometimes to even better effect:

> . . . a dear old white-thatched gentleman who embodies the very spirit of loving-kindness.

Deeper hook:

> This *dear old white-thatched gentleman* happens to be the author of some of the most savage satire . . .

Generally speaking, the last sentence of a paragraph is the best place to find the hook for your new paragraph, for this sentence is the one freshest in the reader's mind. If you go back much deeper than this, you will usually need a multiple hook, as in this example:

> . . . No doubt his photographs have helped promote this image. . . . He looks like . . . the very spirit of loving-kindness.

Multiple hook (still deeper):

> To accept such an *image* is to betray greater familiarity with the *photographs* than with the writing. For Twain wrote some of the most savage satire . . .

Here both *image* and *photographs* are repeated, thus "double hooking" the paragraphs to make up for the greater distance between their first and second appearance. The greater the distance, the more likely you are to need a multiple hook. But no arbitrary rule in this matter is possible. Let your inner ear and your good sense guide you. The important thing is to remember the reader. Make certain that the connection is clear, but don't insult the reader's intelligence by making it too clear—that is, by repeating huge sections or whole sentences from the preceding paragraph. One or two key words will do the job.

All the examples so far have been simple word or phrase, hooks. Another variation of the paragraph hook is the idea

105

hook. The principle is the same; you hook into the preceding paragraph, but instead of repeating an exact word or phrase, you refer to the idea just expressed, compressing it into a single phrase:

> Mark Twain is . . . the very spirit of loving-kindness.

Idea hook:

> *Such a view* of Twain would probably have been a source of high amusement to the author himself. For Twain wrote some of the most savage satire . . .

> or

> Any resemblance between *this popular portrait* and the man who reveals himself in his writing is purely imaginary. For Twain wrote . . .

In neither of the above examples is an exact word or phrase from the first paragraph repeated. But the hook is clearly there; the referential *such a view* and *this popular portrait* fasten the paragraphs firmly together.

The idea hook can be a great deal more subtle than this, of course. If you examine the work of any accomplished essayist, you will find many paragraphs that have no specific word or phrase serving as a link but that are nevertheless unmistakably tied together by meaning. Transitions of this kind require some of the subtlest skills of writing—the ordering of ideas, the use of inference and allusion, the creation of "echo effects," the unobtrusive handling of time and emphasis. All these are skills that derive from an intimate understanding of language—and from experience.

That takes time. Meanwhile, the simple idea hook illustrated above can serve you well. By using it, you can avoid the danger of overloading your work with either the word hooks or the purely mechanical transitions. Any transitional method, remember, can become annoyingly obvious to a reader if it is overused. So vary your practice, never permitting one method of handling transitions to take over the job exclusively.

The Combinations

The combination of standard transitions and paragraph hooks is so natural that you will probably find yourself using it as a matter of course. Any of the samples provided on pages 104, 105, and 106, for example, could be used to demonstrate combinations:

> The *loving-kindness* begins to look a little doubtful, *however,* in view of . . .
>
> *Yet* this *dear old white-thatched gentleman* . . .
>
> *But* to accept such an *image* . . .
>
> *Such a view* of Twain, *however,* would probably . . .

Whether or not to use a single transition or a combination depends partly upon your sense of what the reader requires for clarity and partly upon your view of your material and your natural rhythm in writing. If you are certain that you have made yourself perfectly clear with a single transition, let it stand. If you are not certain, or if the rhythm of the sentence seems to need an extra beat, use the combination.

Summary

Remember that the chief purpose of transitions is to help the reader follow your train of thought. They are the links that hold your ideas together and keep them moving toward a single goal. So make certain, always, that some kind of link exists between your paragraphs, and that the link exists not only in your own mind but also, clearly and unmistakably, in the words you put on paper.

One kind of link is not necessarily better than any other kind, but variety is better than sameness. So try for variety. Use the purely mechanical devices for quick and simple transitions. Use word and phrase hooks for stronger and clearer links. Use idea hooks for broad references. Use combinations for emphasis and tone.

Use them all. But above all, use them.

1. If a paragraph can stand alone as a structure, why should it need to be linked to any other paragraph?
2. Explain the analogy between an essay and a moving train.
3. What are the three kinds of transitions that link paragraphs?
4. Describe a standard transitional device. Give examples.
5. When *however* is used as a transition, what is the best position for it in the sentence?
6. What is the correct punctuation for a tucked-in *however?*
7. This sentence appears on pages 103–104: "You probably use the paragraph hook often in your own writing without knowing it and see it constantly in your reading without realizing it (as in this sentence, for example)." What is the paragraph hook in this sentence? (You will have to look back to the paragraph preceding the sentence for your answer.)
8. Describe the difference between a simple paragraph hook and a deeper hook.
9. What is a multiple hook?
10. How does an idea hook differ from the other kinds of paragraph hooks?
11. What is a combination transition?
12. Is one kind of transition better than any other kind? If so, why? If not, what is the best guide for deciding which kind of transition to use after you have made certain that you are being clear?

ASSIGNMENT

1. In each item below, assume that the first sentence is the opening sentence of a paragraph and that the second sentence is the opening sentence of the next paragraph. Supply a standard transition for the second sentence of each pair.

    a. He received the highest praise for his efforts to

improve living conditions in the slums.
He was frequently criticized.

b. The study of science can be a tremendously exciting intellectual experience.
The study of science can have a narrowing effect.

c. Students are showing greater interest in baseball as a school sport.
Students are showing greater interest in dramatics.

d. The furniture he had acquired for his living room was surely as ugly as anything ever made.
It was comfortable.

e. Far too much emphasis has been placed on psychology and too little on personal responsibility.
A knowledge of psychology can be very valuable.

f. The movie was the victim of poor photography and a bad script.
It was interesting.

2. Insert the word *however* in the second sentence of each pair below.

a. He had taken piano lessons for ten years.
He was not a good pianist.

b. She planned to finish the assignment on Monday.
By Monday she had forgotten all about it.

c. She had very few interests that could be called hobbies.
She liked to take long walks in the city, and these led her eventually to make the city itself her hobby.

d. The council has adopted a wait-and-see attitude.
This is no solution.

3. Write a picture-frame paragraph in which you describe some aspect of your trip to school each morning—perhaps a single city block where you walk, the bus ride through a particular section of town or country, or the attitude of other students you encounter. Then do the following:

a. Write the first sentence of the next paragraph, using a paragraph hook. (You may also include a standard device if you like.)

b. Write another first sentence for your second paragraph, using a deeper hook.

c. Write another first sentence, using a multiple hook.

d. Write another first sentence, using an idea hook.

e. Write a full paragraph, using one of the sentences that you have written as your opening sentence. This will give you two full paragraphs.

f. Write the opening sentence of a third paragraph to follow the two you have just written, using a combination hook for the transition.

VOCABULARY

1. Write a definition for each of the following words:

analogy	indispensable	referential
appropriate *(adj.)*	irrational	sophisticated
arbitrary	multiple	
discreetly	recur	

2. In the left-hand column below are different forms of the words in the vocabulary list. Write a complete sentence in which you use each of these words and also *all* the words and/or phrases that appear opposite it in the right-hand column. This will require a little inventiveness on your part. Your sentence may be as long as you like, and you can fit the combinations into your sentence in any way you please, but hold yourself to one sentence in each case.

a.	analogous	links between paragraphs
b.	appropriately	class, subdued
c.	arbitrarily	time, limited
d.	discreet	information, questions
e.	discretion	allowed, choice
f.	dispense	formality, point
g.	irrationally	convinced, plotting to
h.	multiplying	troubles, blamed, carelessness
i.	recurrent	dream, pursued, who wanted to
j.	reference	understand, background
k.	referring	notes, the impression that
l.	sophistication	dress, contrast, naturalness

110

8

The Passive Voice

In this age of the club and the committee, you have probably listened (or more likely, not listened) at some time in your life to something like this: "The meeting was called to order by the president. The minutes were read. The treasurer's report was given. . . ." And so forth, and so forth, and so forth.

No doubt at this very moment thousands of people, all of them glassy-eyed with boredom, are sitting in a meeting somewhere and listening to a duly-elected secretary read words very much like these. Most of them, including the secretaries, would agree that the minutes of meetings can easily win any contest for the world's dullest writing.

Nobody blames the secretaries; they are simply the victims of a style that has solidified into a convention. Any attempt to change the custom would probably panic the membership. Nor can the meetings themselves be blamed. Sometimes they're interesting. But by the time the proceedings have been put through the "minutes machine," all the interest has been efficiently and thoroughly removed. Even if something really memorable should happen—if an escaped lion, say, should stroll into a committee meeting—the minutes would probably record the event like this:

> The meeting was interrupted by the appearance of a lion. An attempt was made to form a barricade with the furniture. Members were told to remain calm. The police were called. . . .

If you happened to be present at such a meeting, if you had actually found yourself eyeball to eyeball with an uncaged lion—a lion quite possibly on the verge of selecting you for its afternoon snack—you might find this version of the episode a shade inadequate to express your own feelings at the time. You would feel cheated. Judging by those minutes, you might tell a friend resentfully, you'd think nothing at all had happened. A bunch of words has turned something real into something unreal.

Why? How did it happen? What was wrong with the words?

The answer to that question will put you in possession of one of the great secrets of an effective writing style.

Glance again at those sample minutes. They lack suspense, of course, and the kind of detail that helps establish the look and feel of a situation. But something more basic than this is involved; suspense and detail can be added later, after you have located the real trouble. Go straight to the heart of the sentences. Examine the verbs: *was called, were read, was given; was interrupted, was made, were told, were called.* Can these verbs be responsible for the lifelessness, the pervasive dullness, the unrealness of the writing?

They can be, and they are. At bottom, the sentences are lifeless because the verbs are lifeless. And they are lifeless because *they are all in passive voice.*

What It Is, and How to Beat It

The English language has two voices—active voice and passive voice. These terms refer to the use of verbs. Many verbs can be either active or passive, depending upon how

112

you use them. Active voice is direct, vigorous, strong; passive voice is indirect, limp, weak—and sneaky. It can creep unnoticed into your writing unless you are on guard against it constantly and consciously. It is every student's worst enemy, mainly because it is hard to recognize and thus hard to combat. So you must learn quickly and forever the difference between the two voices. Much of your progress from this point forward will depend upon your understanding of this difference. It is that important.

The difference can be quickly and simply illustrated.

Active voice:

> John drove the car.

John is the subject of the sentence, and John *acted*. He did something—he *drove*. The verb shows him in action. Any other sentence with an active verb could demonstrate the same principle: "John likes Mary," "The teacher called the roll," "Joe hit Jimmie." Whenever a verb shows the subject of a sentence *doing something*, the sentence has life.

Now look at the contrast:

Passive voice:

> The car was driven by John.

In this sentence, the subject is *car*. But notice that the car is doing nothing whatever—*it is having something done to it.* You had exactly the same situation in the record of the lion episode: "The meeting was interrupted. . . . An attempt was made. . . . Members were told. . . ." The subjects did not act; they were *acted upon*. Whenever this happens, the sentence is in passive voice.

Perhaps you can see what an extraordinary difference voice can make in style by looking at two versions of a longer sentence:

> Bells were rung, horns were blown, confetti was thrown from every office window, and embraces were exchanged by total strangers.

113

> Bells rang, horns tooted, confetti streamed from every office window, and total strangers threw their arms around each other.

Both sentences say exactly the same thing, but the second version is unquestionably livelier and more interesting than the first. Voice, of course, makes all the difference.

Adrift in Nobody-Land

Perhaps the chief weakness of passive voice is its anonymity. It could almost be called the "nobody" voice:

> The room was cleaned.
> The flowers were cut.
> The lights were turned on.

Who cleaned the room? Who cut the flowers? Who turned on the lights? Who, indeed? Apparently nobody. Ghostly hands have been at work. Everything has taken place in a vacuum; the events seem unreal and shadowy because they lack any sense of human involvement.

This "nobodiness" comes through even when the sentence identifies the actor.

> The room was cleaned by Mary Lou.
> The flowers were cut by Josephine.
> The lights were turned on by Pearlie May.

That added phrase provides information, but it doesn't help the writing. Attaching a live body to an inert, lethargic verb is like putting a rider on a doped horse. The horse—or the sentence—still won't move.

In real life we are bored and exasperated by passivity. When we come into contact with spineless, apathetic people who limply allow themselves to be pushed around, who never make a decision, never respond, never take the initiative, we feel like shaking them up a bit, forcing them to show a little spirit. Complete passivity is unnatural; it offends some basic sense of life in all of us, some insistent demand for human statement and identity.

What bores us in real life bores us no less in writing. And although good manners usually prevent us from shaking some life into passive, listless acquaintances, politeness need not deter us from shaking up our own sentences. In fact, a good way to handle a sentence suffering from passive voice is to cut off its tail and switch it around entirely; in other words, to rewrite it in the active voice:

> The room was cleaned by Mary Lou.
> Mary Lou cleaned the room.
>
> The flowers were cut by Josephine.
> Josephine cut the flowers.
>
> The lights were turned on by Pearlie May.
> Pearlie May turned on the lights.

Notice how the words *by* and *was* (or *were*) disappear? This minor operation is the easiest way to get rid of passive voice.

Making the Subject Perform

It is not always practical to get rid of passive voice by changing the subject of a sentence. "Thunder was heard in the mountains," for example, has no actor, no *by* phrase. Presumably someone heard it, of course. But it would be absurd to supply a "hearer" just so you could eliminate that *was heard.* The result would be something vague and unsatisfactory like "Everybody [*or* many people] heard thunder in the mountains." So leave that thunder where it is. But make it *do* something:

> Thunder *growled* in the mountains.

Now it's in action. It's doing the thing that thunder does. It could also grumble, or mutter, or rumble, or crash, or complain, or snarl, depending upon the kind of thunder-sound you want. The more precise the verb, the more vivid and real the subject becomes. No reader cares in the least about thunder that "was heard." It's real thunder, thunder that we can actually hear, that makes us jump. Thunder that grumbles or snarls is real thunder.

Don't let passive voice steal your thunder. Don't let it steal even the smallest sound. Don't let a tone-deaf verb deaden your sentences. Sound is a sign of life and movement. See what happens in these sentences:

> The sound of dishwashing *was heard*.
> Ella *heard* the sound of dishwashing.
> Dishes *clattered* in the sink.

> The door *was shut* with great force.
> Ella *shut* the door with great force.
> The door *slammed*.

> The motor *was turned on*.
> Ella *turned on* the motor.
> The motor *coughed* into life.

> The room *was filled* with the sudden sound of laughter.
> Ella *heard* the sudden sound of laughter in the room.
> The room *exploded* with laughter.

In every example above, the sentence goes through three stages: It begins with passive voice; it moves into active voice; then it changes structure so that the sound the sentence is trying to communicate reaches us *in the verb,* the active word in the sentence. *Clattered. Slammed. Coughed. Exploded.* We hear the sound directly—not through Ella's ears, but through our own. And the sound is clearly better, more genuinely hearable, when you get it this way, firsthand.

So take advantage of these "soundtrack" verbs whenever possible. Catch the sound at its source, and give it to your reader straight. Everything you write will immediately take on a new and lively sense of reality when you use verbs that transmit an actual sound.

The most powerful of all verbs, however, are those that create *pictures* in the reader's mind. One verb can often bring a whole scene to life. Consider, for example, this limply passive sentence:

> The car was driven down Main Street.

116

You can easily change the sentence to active voice, of course, by providing a driver:

John drove the car down Main Street.

But the verb *drove* is so low-voltage that it's only a step removed from passivity. Make your reader *see* that car; pack a moving picture into your verb:

The car careened down Main Street.

Instantly the car comes into focus. It is no longer merely "going" down Main Street; it is lurching crazily from side to side.

"The car *jolted* down Main Street" supplies a different picture and new information; either the car has a flat or Main Street needs a new paving job. "The car *steamed* down Main Street" shows us a hissing and sputtering car, with a white plume of vapor erupting from its radiator.

The writer need only pick the verb that provides a picture or a sound (or both). Maybe the car *rattled* down Main Street. Or *purred*. Or *whispered*. If the car rattles, it's old and ramshackle and probably ready to fall apart. If it purrs, it is probably new and quite expensive. If it whispers, it is very expensive indeed—a Rolls Royce, perhaps, gleaming black, with a uniformed chauffeur in the front seat and a rich old lady in back. She has come into town to buy fresh liver for her cat. . . .

Such is the power of motion-picture and soundtrack verbs to tease and please the imagination. The more precise the verb, the more vivid the picture and/or sound it creates. The more vivid the picture, the more hearable the sound, the more effective the writing.

Make your subject do something. That's the rule to remember. It will take you out of passive voice, and from that point forward you should experience a steady improvement in style. You will find that forcing a subject to act will bring to your mind verbs that would never have occurred to you otherwise. Your writing will begin to take on some of the power and excitement of direct experience.

That's the highest goal any writer can hope to achieve.

Why Passive Voice at All?

If passive voice is such a menace to style, why not outlaw it altogether? Unfortunately, that's not possible. It's the beginning writer's worst enemy, but it does perform certain limited but necessary functions.

Sometimes, for example, it offers the only way to provide some necessary tone or connotation. It is possible for a verb to be too brisk, too energetic, to express accurately an exact shade of meaning. Or a long series of sentences may seem to need a subtle change in key, a note of softness and distance, simply for contrast. But before allowing yourself to use passive voice, try every possible alternative first. If active voice simply will not work, if you cannot possibly achieve with it the tone or meaning you want, then passive voice is probably right for your purpose.

But look out for tricks. Look out especially for tricking yourself. You will often be tempted to use passive voice because you think it sounds pretty or because it's easier. The passive voice sings a siren song. You'll find yourself praising and defending it at the very moment it is leading you toward the rocks.

In only one respect can passive voice be of positive value. Its very impersonality has a peculiar and special power. Oddly, this meek and colorless voice often provides exactly the right tone for violence and disaster and accident—for any event in which the subject suffers misfortune. "She was hit by a car," for example, certainly conveys the sense of real accident, of the victim's helplessness. "A car hit her" does not; put that way, in fact, it sounds almost absurd. Instinctively, we put disaster in passive voice. The wounded soldier looks at his bleeding arm and says, "I've been hit." When we speak of the man in front of the firing squad, we say he *was shot;* the woman in the burning building *was trapped;* the

118

gangster *was taken* for a ride; the child *was kidnapped.* In each instance the passive voice makes it brutally clear that the subject is not acting but is being acted upon. That, of course, is precisely the effect the writer wants; it carries a sense of shock, of helplessness in the face of calamity.

Occasionally you will find it necessary to use the passive voice for the sake of clarity or to achieve a needed change of tone. In the main, however, passive voice is weak and undesirable. Worse yet, it is habit-forming. Avoid it whenever possible.

A Plan for Self-Protection

As soon as you pick the subject of a sentence, supply it with a verb that makes it *do* something. Never mind about the rest of the sentence; first get that verb. If you don't write it in passive voice, you won't have to change it. (This is known as the "cut-it-off-at-the-pass" technique.)

But keep your guard up. Passive voice can slip into a sentence so smoothly that you never see it enter. If you start looking for it, it melts into the background. If you find it, it has a way of looking touchingly innocent, thus persuading you to leave it alone. Don't be fooled. Get rid of it.

The best way to avoid passive voice, yet still have it on hand when absolutely necessary, is to follow these four steps:

　　1. If you use a passive verb, try to change it.

　　2. If you can't change it, try a new sentence.

　　3. If that doesn't work, try skipping the sentence altogether.

　　4. As a last resort, use passive voice.

One final warning: The passive voice has two extremes. At one end is secretarial prose. That's the easiest one to fight because it's so obvious. At the other end is a kind of prose perhaps best classified as vaguely poetic. At this extreme, passive voice acquires a peculiar aura of its own, a subtle undertone of "Ah how sweet and sad and strange the world is" (always pleasing to the young, and to the young writer almost irresistible). Resist it.

Summary

Training yourself to spot the passive voice in your writing and to put it to rout can be an immensely valuable discipline. It not only will push you toward more direct and forceful statement but will give you a sharper awareness of language as a flexible instrument, a thing of movable parts that responds to experiment and adjusts to new patterns. Above all, an attack on passive voice will open up vast new resources of power available in verbs.

Passive voice will always have certain important uses, but remember that you must keep your eye on it all the time or it will drop its *o* and change swiftly from passive voice to passive vice. You must learn to outwit it. *Make your subject perform.* Adopt that as your guiding principle, and you can vanquish one of your most insidious enemies. Only after you have conquered passive voice can you return to it with confidence, knowing when to use it—and why.

So discipline yourself. Put a deliberate check on your tendency to drift into the passive. Experiment with new arrangements of words. Reach for the precise and vivid verb. Make those sentences move. Then you can be sure they are alive.

QUESTIONS

1. How does the relationship between subject and verb differ in active and passive voice? Give examples.
2. What is meant by the phrase "a style that has solidified into a convention"?
3. Why is a *by* phrase frequently a sign of passive voice?
4. How can you convert a sentence containing a *by* phrase from passive to active voice?
5. What is a soundtrack verb? Give examples not taken from this chapter.

6. According to an old Chinese proverb, one picture is worth more than ten thousand words. How could you apply this proverb to writing?
7. What one rule will help you avoid passive voice?
8. Under what circumstances is passive voice more effective than active voice?
9. What is the cut-it-off-at-the-pass technique in reference to passive voice?

ASSIGNMENT

1. Make a list, in the order of their appearance, of all the passive verbs in the following paragraph:

> A man was seen at the intersection, calmly crossing against the light. Cars were brought to a shrieking halt. Horns were honked. Warnings were shouted by the crowd waiting on the corner, and in the distance a series of small crashes could be heard from the growing line of cars as bumpers were engaged unexpectedly. None of this was noticed by the man, a narrow-chested little fellow in a black suit. A black briefcase was carried in one hand and a rolled umbrella in the other. When the opposite side of the intersection was reached, his umbrella was raised in a brief salute to the cars that were now hopelessly stalled for blocks because of him. Then he was seen no more.

2. Rewrite the paragraph in active voice, rearranging the sentences in any way you like in order to create a smooth sequence.
3. Write an original paragraph describing something you saw yesterday. It can be an event you witnessed or simply an object you observed. It need not be important or exciting, but it must be something real described as completely as possible. Use passive voice only.
4. Rewrite your paragraph in active voice.
5. Write a complete essay with a thesis based on the general subject of passive voice. Make any point you like, but use the two paragraphs you wrote for 3 and 4 above as examples to illustrate your point.

1. Find a definition for each of the following words:

anonymity	initiative	memorable
apathetic	insidious	pervasive
aura	irresistible	vacuum
convention	lethargic	vanquish

2. Finish each of the incomplete sentences below so that it will demonstrate your understanding of the meaning of the italicized word.

   a. On a large college campus students often suffer from a sense of *anonymity*. They feel that . . . , that . . . , and that . . .

   b. Response to the athletic program last year was *apathetic* at best. Students either . . . or . . .

   c. Her nominating speech certainly did not follow the standard *convention*. Instead of . . . she . . .

   d. In the campaign to improve living conditions in the refugee camp, John Fletcher took the *initiative*. He was not the kind of man who could . . .

   e. To her the appeal of the sea was *irresistible*. She felt . . . and she . . .

   f. He felt completely *lethargic*. He could not . . . What he wanted above all else was . . .

   g. It was a *memorable* moment. For the first time in her life she . . . , and she knew . . .

   h. The peculiar scent in the house, reminiscent of both roses and mildew, was faint but *pervasive*. It clung to . . . , emanated from . . . , and seemed to be part of . . .

   i. The man's mind seemed to be a complete *vacuum*. He seemed incapable of . . . , and he . . .

   j. Nothing could *vanquish* his high spirits. Even when . . . , he . . .

9

The Sound of Sentences

So long ago that you have probably forgotten how or where it happened, you discovered that you could talk—not just pronounce a few words but string them together and thus express whole thoughts. This miraculous discovery may have taken place very early indeed, perhaps while you were still taking your meals in a high chair and getting things like chopped spinach for lunch—whereupon you probably said, in the manner of any sensible child, "I don't want spinach. I want cookies." If this announcement had no immediate effect on your menu, it at least had dazzling implications for your future. For you were suddenly talking in sentences.

At that age, of course, you had no idea they were called sentences. They were simply sounds—long, satisfying sounds with a solid feeling of beginning, middle, and end. Nobody had to tell you when you had those sounds right. Your own ear took care of that.

Then you learned to read sentences and finally to write them. You may even remember the day you produced your first piece of writing. Clutching a thick lead pencil and biting your lower lip, you managed to copy a set of mysterious symbols that spelled out something more or less like this:

> Sally saw the cat.
> It was a big cat.
> It was a black cat.
> It was a big, black cat.

Here, you were told, were Sentences. You had been gabbling happily for several years, of course, in sentences of your own that were far more complicated than these, and certainly more interesting. But you didn't know that. Obviously, if these things on your paper were sentences, then sentences were something entirely different from talk. The proof lay on your desk in front of you: "Sally saw the cat. It was a big cat. It was a black cat. . . ." You were sure that these idiocies couldn't be talk. And you were right.

But you learned, obediently, what you had to learn: that sentences started with a capital letter and ended with a period, that *Sally* was a noun, *saw* was a verb, *big* was an adjective. You probably learned, in addition, a few things that weren't strictly a part of the lesson. You learned to hate Sally. You learned to hate Sally's cat. And you learned to hate sentences. If sentences were this kind of stuff, who wanted them?

Indeed, nobody. But that was something else you couldn't know. So you grew up believing that spoken sentences sounded one way and written sentences another. Written sentences, you were firmly convinced, not only sounded different but were *supposed* to sound different. You learned eventually that some of the sentences you found in print seemed almost as easy and natural as talk, but you couldn't quite shake your own sentences free. Sally and that cat were still prowling through your subconscious, putting a stop to any idea of relaxing your guard. You had the uneasy feeling that it was dangerous, even faintly immoral, to put a sentence in writing until you had starched and stiffened and sterilized it beyond any resemblance to natural speech.

That, at any rate, is one theory—admittedly unscientific, but not altogether unserious—to explain the central problem facing most students in their writing. And that problem is not grammar or spelling or any kind of formal "correctness." These things, to be sure, may be problems, but they are almost entirely separate from the real problem, which is how to write sentences that sound as natural and effortless as talk.

To solve the problem, you must outwit Sally and her cat. You must realize that writing is, in the final analysis, a form of talk—preserved talk, talk that has been caught in flight and pinned down on paper so that the words can be heard again. Heard, mind you—not merely seen. For clinging to every piece of writing is the sound of the writer's voice, the human sound of one person speaking to others. The sound of that voice registers instantly on a reader's inner ear—registers so strongly, in fact, that it is probably true to say that reading is almost as much an act of hearing as of seeing.

When you put a book down because you find it dull or difficult, because you "simply can't read it" or "can't keep your mind on it," it is not your eyes that object to the printed word. It's your ear, objecting to the *sound* of the printed words—that inner ear which demands from all written words the sound of a human voice. It's the same ear that told you, in the first or second grade, that the story of Sally and her cat was boring and silly.

Nobody talked like that, and you knew it.

But if writing should sound like talk, it would appear at first glance very easy to write sentences with the right sound simply by talking first and writing later—transferring the spoken words to paper exactly as spoken. Theoretically, this should result in a sound of absolute naturalness. But here you run into the great paradox of writing: Written sentences should *sound* like natural speech, but they can't *be* natural speech.

The reasons for this are fairly obvious. Natural speech is a great deal more than words. In fact, it depends for most of its effect upon a great number of things that can't be put on paper: tone of voice, facial expressions, body movements, rate of speed, manner, even the speaker's appearance. Strip all these things away, leaving only the words—as you must when you transfer spoken language, exactly as spoken, to paper—and the words seem completely flat.

In any case, natural speech is far too disorganized, too repetitive, too careless to stand up under the kind of examination it would get in print. Even the most brilliant spoken language tends to flatten into ordinariness when it is converted to written words. So no piece of writing can be defended on the basis of "That's the way I really talk." The whole point of writing is to create something a great deal better than the way you "really" talk—a great deal more interesting, more thoughtful, more effective in every way— but to make it *sound* as natural and effortless as talk.

It begins to look impossible. Your voice, your face, your gestures can't help you. The actual words of speech can't help you. What's left? Only one thing—the *rhythm* of speech. This is the one thing you can borrow from it, the one thing you *must* borrow if your written words are ever to achieve an air of naturalness.

The Rhythm of Speech

All spoken language, no matter who the speaker may be or what the subject is, has a natural rhythm. You will hear this rhythm wherever you hear talk: in your best friend's conversation, in a salesperson's pitch, in a math teacher's explanation of a problem, in an impromptu speech at a club meeting, in your father's or mother's reading of the riot act.

Compare the two short paragraphs below.

> Example A:
> I want that car back here by ten o'clock. And when I say ten o'clock, I don't mean ten-thirty or ten-fifteen or ten-five. I mean *ten*. You remember that. Because I'm telling you right now, this is the last time you drive that car if you come home late again. And that's *final*.

> Example B:
> One of the things that is very important to an actor is a sense of timing. It is more important than a handsome

126

face or a good voice. An actor who does not have a sense of timing can never be very good at acting. A good director can tell him what to do, but he will always be just like a puppet.

As they stand now, the two examples have nothing whatever in common. The first is quite obviously *spoken* language. It's completely natural, but it is certainly not suitable for use in an essay. The second example is quite obviously *not* spoken language; you identify it instantly as a written paragraph, probably from a student essay (which it is). You may feel that the second paragraph is more "dignified" than the first (actually, it is not—it's merely duller). In any case, the two paragraphs are so completely different—in approach, in tone, in subject matter—that it would appear impossible to transfer anything at all from one to the other.

Yet something can be transferred. Perhaps you can discover for yourself what it is by examining the paragraph below. It makes exactly the same point it made originally (in Example B, above) but makes it better. And in one respect it is now exactly like Example A. See if you can detect what it is. that the two paragraphs now have in common.

Few things are so essential to an actor as a sense of timing. Without that, nothing else about him matters very much. He may have a handsome face. He may have a splendid voice. But unless he has an innate sense of timing, the finest director in the world cannot make an actor of him. He can never be more than a puppet.

The meaning of the paragraph has not changed. It doesn't take a great ear for language, however, to realize that this second version is far more effective as a piece of writing than the first. It is more effective because *the sentences now have the natural rhythm of speech.* In fact, the rhythm of this paragraph is a deliberate repetition of the rhythm of the parent's natural speech.

Make a sentence-by-sentence comparison of sentence length. The six sentences in both passages are matched for length. The parent's speech happened to fall in a pattern of medium-medium-short-short-long-short, so the second paragraph was matched to that pattern. Both paragraphs could now be "graphed" like this:

The fact that the sentence lengths in the two passages are now exactly alike is unimportant except as a demonstration of how easily sentences can be adjusted to "sound right." The important thing to remember is that the length of sentences in all speech is always erratic, always changing. *The first principle of rhythm in writing, to capture the basic rhythm of speech, is variation of sentence length.*

Furthermore, the mere act of forcing yourself to vary the length of sentences will force you simultaneously to change their structure and therefore their wording—always for the better. Glance again at the first version of Example B. Notice that every sentence is almost exactly the same length. And as frequently happens when length does not vary, almost every sentence has the same monotonous structure. These are nothing but *Sally-cat* sentences, grown up and pretending to be dignified, but nevertheless *Sally-cat*. And your ear rebels for the same reason it rebelled in the first grade: nobody talks like that.

So write with a talking rhythm, varying the length of your sentences to suit your material. Generally the short, sharp sentence gives emphasis; the long, involved sentence provides depth and color. Together with the medium-length sentence, they give writing the tone and rhythm of speech. Put them in any order you like. Any order is right if it sounds right to your own inner ear. Write for that ear.

If you find it difficult at first to "hear" your sentences, just use your eyes. If your sentences are all approximately the same length, vary them arbitrarily. Cut a sentence down here, extend another one there, join two together, or split a long one in half. Gradually you will find your own voice, discover your own particular rhythm.

Getting Inside the Sentence

So far you have been concerned with the broad rhythms of sentences, with the effect of a variety of sentence lengths. Now it is time to look at individual sentences. For although the first step toward achieving a "talking rhythm" in writing is through variation in sentence length, a great deal more is involved than length alone. It is not enough merely to make a sentence longer or shorter; you must also make it *better*.

It's a great deal easier to write a good short sentence than a good long one, of course, for in making it short you will instinctively cut it down to its most important parts. Take this example:

> In general, it can be said that things have a tendency
> to happen this way in a person's own experience.

Chop the undergrowth out of that jungle and you are down to essentials:

> That's life.
>   or
> Life is like that.

The real problems begin when you write longer sentences. You can make a sentence longer, after all, simply by adding a few meaningless phrases or by repeating in slightly different words what you have already said. The only thing this does for a dull sentence is to make it duller.

> One of the things that is very important to an actor
> is a sense of timing, because a sense of timing is
> something every actor must have.

The sentence is certainly longer (compare it to the original on page 126), but it is now worse than dull—it's downright simple-minded. You might justifiably conclude either that (1) the writer was a moron or (2) the writer considered you, the reader, to be a moron—and neither conclusion would make you feel very friendly.

You can, of course, make a sentence longer simply by joining it to another sentence with a connective word. Sometimes this works. But very often it doesn't. In fact, it can throw a whole paragraph out of kilter, as you can easily prove for yourself by trying to join any two sentences in the example on page 127 with *and* or any other conjunction. Or consider the disaster of joined *Sally-cat* sentences:

> Sally saw the cat, and it was a big cat, and it was a black cat; in other words, it was a big, black cat.

This is an extreme of simple-mindedness, of course, but at least it serves as a warning against thoughtless splices.

But, you may say, the *Sally-cat* sentences were hopeless from the start, and it is unfair to use them as examples. Is it? "Sally saw the cat" is a perfectly legitimate sentence—the very model, in fact, of the simple sentence: subject, verb, object. "John loves Mary," "The garden needs rain," "Lightning struck the tree," "The car hit the lamp post." These are all simple sentences. And they all can be made longer, more involved and interesting, including Sally's:

> Sally, caught by a sudden movement at the window, a movement so silent that she thought for a moment she had seen the shadow of a passing bird, finally saw the big black cat.

That's only one of an almost limitless number of ways that the sentence could be changed from short to long. But it is enough to demonstrate two things: (1) To make a sentence longer, you must provide additional material of some kind. (2) The additional material should blend smoothly with the main part of the sentence, seeming a natural part of its growth. Note that the added material in the example above—*caught by a sudden movement, a movement so silent that . . .* —is firmly secured *inside* the sentence, hemmed in by *Sally* at one end and *saw* at the other. Thus the sentence

130

grows from within, and its skin stretches naturally and easily to accommodate its expanding middle.

This expansion from within creates an extremely solid sentence, an all-of-a-piece structure with no loose ends. But such sentences should be alternated with looser, less formally constructed sentences for the sake of variety. You can make a sentence longer simply by adding detail to it *after* the basic statement:

> Sally saw the cat, immense, velvety black, regally indifferent to her presence, its unblinking green stare as remote and self-possessed as an emperor's.

Details that are properly handled will never seem like hastily contrived bits and pieces pinned to the end of a sentence simply to make it longer; they will seem like a natural extension, part of the whole growing process.

But enough of Sally and the cat; now that they have served the useful purpose of proving that no sentence is ever really hopeless, they can be left behind. Your own sentences will be much easier to work with, simply because they are your own—and because they will have the strength and purpose of a central idea.

The Basic Statement

In view of the staggering variety of sentences you encounter in a day's reading, you might think that sentences could have a hundred or even a thousand different patterns. Actually, they have only two of major importance: (1) the strung-along sentence and (2) the periodic sentence.

Every sentence in the English language will fit into one of these categories or will be a combination of both.* And once you understand the two patterns, you can write any kind of sentence you like—whether one word or one hundred words long—without the slightest fear of going off the rails.

---

*One such combination, the "balanced sentence," is treated in the next chapter as part of the study of parallel structure.

You can master these patterns easily (they are surprisingly simple, once you learn to recognize them) if you first get a grip on one important principle—the principle of the *basic statement.*

All the following are basic statements:

> Bells rang.
> Love is blind.
> The cat scratched Sally.
> John gave his mother flowers.
> The teacher considered him a good student.

These are basic statements because you cannot remove one word from any of them without damaging or destroying the meaning. They are pure, distilled extract-of-sentence, containing everything they need to make a complete statement and absolutely nothing else.

Every English sentence contains a basic statement. It may stand alone as one short sentence (as in the examples above), or it may be buried inside a longer sentence. But it is always present, it is always complete, and it is irreducible. It's the thing you have left after you chop away everything in a sentence except its essential meaning. And it's the thing you build on when you want to make a sentence longer.

You cannot subtract from a basic statement; you can only add to it. And you can add to it in two major ways. Those two ways are represented in the strung-along sentence and the periodic sentence.

The Strung-along Sentence

The strung-along, or loose, sentence is simply the basic statement with a string of details added at the beginning or the end. The string can be as long or as short as you care to make it. The basic statement does not change:

Basic statement:
> Bells rang.

Strung-along sentence:

> Bells rang, *filling the air with their clangor, startling pigeons into flight from every belfry, bringing people into the streets to hear the news.*

Basic statement:

> The teacher considered him a good student.

Strung-along sentence:

> The teacher considered him a good student, *steady if not eager, responsive to instruction, and conscientious about his work.*

Any basic statement can be converted to a strung-along sentence by the addition of detail. For another example, look at the description of the cat on page 131.

The Periodic Sentence

This is the sentence in which additional details are added *inside* the basic statement. That basic statement is a tight little structure; it must be broken in two at some point and spread apart to make room for added cargo. Details are dropped into the space between the two parts:

Basic statement:

> Love is blind.

Periodic sentence:

> Love, *as everyone knows except those who happen to be afflicted with it,* is blind.

Basic statement:

> John gave his mother flowers.

Periodic sentence:

> John, *the tough one, the sullen kid who scoffed at any show of sentiment,* gave his mother flowers.

Delay, of course, is the secret weapon of the periodic sentence. By holding off the final words of the basic statement until the last possible moment, the sentence builds its own small feeling of suspense. And readers are carried along almost irresistibly to the end, for exactly the same

133

reason they are carried along by a mystery story—because they want to know "how it comes out."

The periodic is the most artful of all sentences. Its structure has a kind of natural elegance, an air of perfectly controlled movement, of assured grace. Its structure is so distinctive, in fact, that it is not wise to place too many pure periodic sentences too close together. Space them out with the looser, strung-along variety and with small, tight sentences, for contrast. Otherwise they will call attention to themselves. But an occasional periodic sentence can add richness and tension to writing that may otherwise seem too loose and casual.

The Combinations

Once you have learned to recognize and use the two major sentence patterns, you can forget about adhering strictly to the pure strung-along or pure periodic model. Your best sentences are likely to combine elements of both.

Again the ear must rule—and the ear must be attuned to the sound of the full paragraph. A perfectly patterned sentence may have a splendid ring when it is considered alone, but it may not join smoothly with the other sentences around it. In that case, adjust it. Add to it, subtract from it, juggle it this way and that; if it ceases to be a pure example of one particular pattern, who cares? The important thing is that it should sound right in relation to the sentences on either side of it.

Suppose you are working with a short, simple sentence—a sentence reduced to the barest basic statement:

John was angry.

That may sound exactly right inside your paragraph—just short enough and sharp enough to have the force you want. In that case, leave it alone. But perhaps that nagging inner ear tells you that it isn't quite right; it needs something. So you make it a shade periodic:

John was *suddenly, violently* angry.

Or you make it even more periodic:

> John, *usually the calmest of men,* was *suddenly, violently* angry.

Or you decide to add detail at the end:

> John, *usually the calmest of men,* was *suddenly, violently* angry, *so angry that he lost control completely.*

Now the sentence is both periodic and loose. You could shake it up still more by moving some of the detail up front:

> *Usually the calmest of men,* John was *suddenly, violently* angry, *so angry that . . .*

The whole point is to take advantage of the flexibility of sentences, changing the pattern constantly in order to avoid monotony. In case you have the mistaken notion that a sentence is flexible only if it has a high emotional charge (John, certainly, was in a state before we got through with him), observe a calmer sentence in the process of change:

Basic statement:

> Too many students work only for grades.

Periodic sentence:

> Too many students, *obsessed with the idea that education is a contest,* work only for grades.

Periodic and loose combined:

> Too many students, *obsessed with the idea that education is a contest,* work only for grades, *forgetting—or never realizing—that learning is not a race to be won but an adventure to be enjoyed.*

> or

> *Obsessed with the idea that education is a contest,* too many students work only for grades . . .

In short, any sentence that goes beyond basic statement is a thing of movable parts, regardless of content. So move the parts. Combine and recombine, shift and change, add and subtract. Shuffle the parts around until you have exactly the shade of emphasis you want. Experiment. Nobody can tell you in advance exactly how to order the parts; too much depends upon the sound of the sentence in relation to those around it.

Listen to your sentences. Consult your inner ear. Ask yourself constantly: "Does this sound right? Does it blend smoothly and logically with the sentences around it? Does it vary enough in structure to avoid monotony?" If it doesn't, move in. Start shoving those words and phrases around until that inner ear approves.

Selecting the Details

Most students grasp easily the technique of adding details to a sentence. What stumps them is the job of actually making up the details. They know *how* to add but not *what* to add. Faced with the necessity of filling out with detail a sentence they have already labored long to produce, they respond with a gloomy and hopeless, "I can't think of another thing."

If you count yourself among this despairing crew, it's time you realized that every time you say you "can't think of another thing" you are talking nonsense. Think "house." Your mind swarms with rooflines, windows, rooms, furniture, colors, noises, smells, seasons, streets, lawns, plaster, plumbing, porches, pets, and people. Think "ran." Instantaneously your mind recreates the sound of pounding feet and straining breath, the feel of the wind on your face or the stitch in your side, the sense of panic or pleasure that accompanied the running. Think "dog," think "book," think "popularity," think anything you like. You will always think of other things as well. The truth is that you can't *not* think of other things; it is humanly impossible.

Your own mind—every human being's mind—is a giant memory bank storing bits and pieces of everything you have experienced, everything you have ever seen or touched or tasted or smelled or heard or thought or felt. Certainly you have forgotten a great many things, but the wealth of detail still on tap is inexhaustible. Short of cutting off your head, you couldn't get rid of these memories even if you wanted to. So don't worry about being in short supply when it comes to details. You have your own private bank overflowing with them. All you need is a key to the vaults.

Any word in any basic statement can be the key (excepting only words like *the* and *a* and *but* and *yet,* which have no counterpart in real life). Suppose that you must add detail to this sentence:

> The class read the assignment.

Immediately you have three words that have literally hundreds of associations in your mind: *class, read, assignment* (subject, verb, object). Any one of them, or all of them, can be enriched and extended.

Not all sentences, of course, have this simple subject-verb-object structure, for not every verb takes a direct object. For your purposes, that doesn't matter. You need not know the precise grammatical terms for all the elements in a sentence in order to work with those elements. The important thing to remember is that the subject, the verb, and *anything that follows the verb* can be expanded.

Start with the subject.

Expanding the Subject

The easiest way to start the details flowing is to think of the subject as being followed by a pause. Make yourself hear that pause. It is exactly the same kind of pause that occurs in your own conversation every day, in sentences like this:

> "That boy, the one wearing glasses, is in my history class."
> "My mother, after all this time, says I can't go."
> "This piecrust, tough as it is, tastes pretty good."

Boy and *mother* and *piecrust* hang in the air, waiting for something more to be said about them. Exactly the same principle applies to a written sentence:

> The class [*pause*] read the assignment.

If you make yourself hear that pause, it will drive you to say something more about the class.

To prime the pump, ask yourself questions about the class: "What kind of class is it? What is its attitude? How does it behave? Where does it meet? What is the most outstanding thing about it? What word or words would you use to describe it?" You can't answer all these questions in the pause after the word *class,* of course, but you can pick out the answer that is most relevant, perhaps one of these:

1. The class, *a mixture of juniors and seniors in advanced math,* . . .

2. The class, *usually noisy and inattentive,* . . .

3. The class, *alarmed by the prospect of an early test,* . . .

4. The class, *apathetic at best but frozen now into attitudes of complete boredom,* . . .

5. The class, *with a subdued rustle of books and papers,* . . .

6. The class, *settling easily into its new quarters in the annex,* . . .

7. The class, *after trying unsuccessfully to divert Mr. Dunwiddy into a discussion of the football game,* . . .

For the sake of variety, the additions should occasionally appear ahead of the subject:

With a subdued rustle of books and papers, the class . . .

After trying unsuccessfully to divert Mr. Dunwiddy into a discussion of the football game, the class . . .

The ear rules, as usual. Whether you put the new material in front of the subject or behind it depends entirely upon your personal preference.

As a rule, picture-and-sound-effect details, or details that suggest feeling (*alarmed at the prospect*), are the most effective. On this basis, Sentence 1 above is the weakest: "The class, *a mixture of juniors and seniors . . .*" That's straight fact, conveying neither picture nor sound and without a hint of atmosphere. This sort of substitute subject is called an *appositive*. It means the same thing as *class;* you could drop *class* and write "The mixture of juniors and seniors read the assignment." The appositive is a convenient and straightforward method of identification that you will use often, but you can nearly always improve it by adding an adjective to suggest an additional shade of meaning: *a lethargic mixture, a lively mixture, an uneasy mixture.*

Graphic details are more interesting than plain appositives—and more fun to write. Three ways to make details graphic are shown in the examples on page 138. You can use an adjective (*noisy, inattentive, apathetic*), a prepositional phrase (*with a subdued rustle*), or a verb form (*alarmed, frozen, settling, trying*). The ones using a verb form are usually the most effective, simply because they carry a hint of action. Verbs are so powerful that even in a subordinate position like this, held down to half their strength, they carry a big jolt of energy.

But don't stick to any one method of adding to your subject. Switch from one to the other. Combine them. Notice that all three work together in Sentence 4—the adjective and the verb form are combined with prepositional phrases:

> The class, *apathetic at best but frozen now into attitudes of complete boredom,* . . .

The possibilities for combination are practically limitless. You could even combine a straight appositive with the other elements in the example above, if you felt like it.

You may have noticed that each example on page 138 employs a slightly different principle in its presentation of detail. At the end of this chapter you will find exercises based on these examples; they will familiarize you quickly with the various methods.

Expanding the Verb

You can expand the verb by showing how the action of the verb progresses:

> The class read, *listlessly at first, and then with growing interest,* the *day's* assignment.

Notice that *day's* has been slipped in ahead of *assignment.* Somehow *assignment* all by itself seemed bare and inadequate; the rhythm demanded the extra word (read the sentence over aloud to see whether you agree). An additional phrase describing the assignment would probably be better yet. Added weight in a verb section often demands more weight at some other point.

Any phrase that tells how or when a verb acts is, of course, related grammatically to the verb, not to the subject or the object. But it's often easier to think of a how-or-when phrase while you are working with the subject, as in Sentence 7:

> The class, *after trying unsuccessfully to divert Mr. Dunwiddy into a discussion of the football game,* read the assignment.

Obviously, it's the reading and not the class that came "after." But the example is included under methods of adding detail to the subject rather than the verb simply because you are most likely to think of it at that point. And certainly it sounds better after *class* than it would sound after *read.* (Try reading it aloud both ways if you doubt this.)

Or you could even add the phrase after the object:

> The class read the assignment, *after trying unsuccessfully . . .*

You needn't worry about the grammatical distinctions. Just look at your verb, ask yourself how you can add to it by describing how or when it happened, and let the new material fall where it makes sense and sounds right. The grammar will take care of itself.

Expanding the Rest of the Sentence

The simplest way to expand the rest of the sentence is to look for its most important noun (often this will be a direct object) and follow it with an appositive—a word or phrase that means the same thing:

I saw Mr. Hassenfeffer, *the manager.*
The class read the assignment, *a full chapter.*

The appositive, of course, simply provides additional identification for the word preceding it, making it more specific.

Sometimes a simple appositive is all you need (depending, as usual, upon the demand of your ear for rhythm). But often you will want to add more than that, and you can give your sentence more interest by adding details to the appositive. For example:

1. I saw Mr. Hassenfeffer, *the manager, a huge man ·with a flattened nose and beady eyes.*

2. The class read the assignment, *a full chapter with a dismaying number of difficult-looking statistical tables.*

3. I saw Mr. Hassenfeffer, *the manager, flat-nosed, beady-eyed, on guard every minute.*

4. The class read the assignment, *a full chapter, dull, difficult, statistics-packed.*

5. I saw Mr. Hassenfeffer, *the manager, who gave me one alert, suspicious glance and then ignored me.*

6. The class read the assignment, *a full chapter so crowded with statistics that most of the students were ready to give up in despair before the end of the period.*

7. I saw Mr. Hassenfeffer, *the manager, waving his arms like a madman and turning slowly purple.*

8. The class read the assignment, *a full chapter covering trade relations before the war and containing a dismaying number of statistical tables.*

Notice the heavy use of prepositional phrases in all the additions in these examples: *with a flattened nose . . . ,with a dismaying number, of . . . statistical tables, on guard,* and so forth. This is characteristic. In fact, one way to help yourself think of additional details is to add a preposition that forces you to ask a question: "I saw Mr. Hassenfeffer, *the manager, a huge man with . . .*" "With what?" your mind asks, and you are driven to answer: *with red whiskers, with a bulging briefcase, with a reputation for scaring the wits out of new employees. With* is usually the best one to start the details rolling. Others follow: *a full chapter with* (with what?) . . . *with a dismaying number of* (of what?) . . . *of statistical tables on* (on what?) . . . *on trade relations*—and so forth, almost endlessly.

It is a mistake, however, to stick only to prepositional phrases when you expand an object (or any other noun that comes after the verb). Notice that Sentences 5–8 contain verb forms of various sorts. In Sentences 7 and 8 they go straight from the noun (*manager, chapter*) into a verb form (*waving, covering*). Semiverbs like this are called *participles.* They have enough verb energy to add life to a descriptive passage.

You can also, of course, convert prepositional phrases into shorter phrases or single words as in Sentence 3: *Flat-nosed, beady-eyed* instead of *with a flattened nose and beady eyes.* It's a good idea to telescope a prepositional phrase into one descriptive word whenever possible, and placing the descriptive word or words after the noun instead of ahead of it adds considerable zest because it upsets the usual word pattern. *The manager, flat-nosed, beady-eyed* sounds, for some reason, much more sinister than *The flat-nosed, beady-eyed manager.* The point here is not to use one word pattern to the exclusion of another but to vary them constantly, remembering that an unusual pattern is likely to give special emphasis.

Summary

Written sentences should have the sound of speech—intelligent, highly ordered speech that sounds completely natural to the listening inner ear of the reader. The means to this naturalness is through variety in sentence patterns: basic statements, strung-along sentences, periodic sentences, combinations. By learning to add detail in various ways to a basic statement, you can create any of these patterns; and by alternating them, by striving consciously for variety, by listening to your sentences as well as looking at them, you can create the natural cadence of the human voice.

The big obstacle that most student writers must overcome is the conviction that any sentence, once written, is an immovable and unchangeable object, like a chunk of concrete or an engraving on steel. You must remember that a sentence is a thing of movable parts, an endlessly adaptable structure that is completely subject to the writer's will, shrinking or expanding to fit the sound and sense the writer chooses to give it.

So relax. Loosen up. Play boldly with sentences. Combine, convert, shift, change, add, subtract, divide. Take chances. The more you experiment, the more you will learn.

QUESTIONS

1. Why is a child likely to believe that written sentences have nothing to do with spoken language?
2. In what sense is reading "almost as much an act of hearing as of seeing"?
3. Written sentences should sound like natural speech but cannot actually be natural speech. Explain.
4. What is the first principle of rhythm in writing?
5. What is a basic statement?
6. Describe the difference between a strung-along sentence and a periodic sentence.
7. What are the three main places in a sentence that can be expanded by details?
8. Name three ways of constructing graphic details, illustrating each method with an example not taken from the text.
9. How do you add details to a verb?
10. What is an appositive? Give an example. How can a preposition help you to think of details to add to an appositive?

1. Reduce all the following sentences to basic statements:

   a. Looking from the mountain road above like a small tumble of children's toys left carelessly behind on the desert floor, the village slept in the sun, its streets empty, its houses shuttered and silent.
   b. The old man ate noisily, making a great clatter with his silverware, blowing on his coffee, smacking his lips with pleasure.
   c. Whatever else he may have been, however rude or quarrelsome or untidy, he was honest in all his dealings in every way.
   d. As he left the town behind, he gained speed, pushing the little car faster and faster through the flat countryside that stretched endlessly to right and left of a highway as smooth and flat as the blade of a knife.
   e. The telephone rang, its shrill summons bringing everybody in the room to frightened attention.

2. Write a strung-along sentence at least twenty words long using each of the basic statements below as a starting point. Do not change the basic statement; just add to it. (See examples, pages 132–133.)

   a. The moon rose.
   b. The man was dead.
   c. He longed to be free.
   d. She liked the song.
   e. They had a good time.

3. Using each of the basic statements below, write five periodic sentences at least fifteen words long. (See examples, page 133.)

   a. Mary left the room.
   b. The world's greatest invention is the safety pin.
   c. Hate is based on fear.
   d. The man was dead.
   e. The circus was his life.

4. Select five of the ten sentences you have just written and add details that will make each one a combination of strung-along and periodic.

5. Expand the subject of the sentence below in the seven different ways illustrated on page 138. Follow the patterns exactly.

> The old man shuffled out of sight.

6. Expand the verb of each of the following sentences.

    a. The girl walked across the playground.
    b. The boy talked about fishing.

7. Add a simple appositive to the noun at the end of each sentence below:

    a. He liked the car.
    b. John read the book.
    c. They listened to the lecture.
    d. It was a special chair.
    e. He called the dog.

8. Using both prepositional phrases and participles, add detail to each of the appositives in the five sentences you have just written. Make each sentence at least fifteen words long.

9. Add an appositive and a *who* clause to the sentence below, following the pattern shown in Sentence 5, page 141.

> They asked for Mrs. Smith.

10. Write a sentence containing an appositive and a *so . . . that* comparison as shown in Sentence 6, page 141.

VOCABULARY

1. Define each of the following words:

adhering	implication	paradox
arbitrarily	inexhaustible	repetitive
erratic	irreducible	sinister
exorcised	obstacle	subconscious

2. Below are the first few words of six incomplete sentences. Finish each of the sentences, using all the following:

(1) the word shown in parentheses with each; (2) an appositive; and (3) at least one prepositional phrase. The three items need not be used in the order given here, but all three must appear in each sentence.

    a. Although John had worked out a . . .
       (adhering)
    b. He managed to . . .   (arbitrarily)
    c. The rhythm of . . .   (erratic)
    d. The ghosts . . .   (exorcised)
    e. We can only guess at . . .   (implication)
    f. The resources of . . .   (inexhaustible)

3. Follow each of the statements below with a second statement that explains the first in different words.

    a. A basic statement is irreducible; . . .
    b. Writing that sounds natural is a paradox; . . .
    c. The speaker was needlessly repetitive; . . .
    d. His fear was subconscious; . . .

10

Parallel Structure

Parallel structure, fully understood and put to use, can bring about such a startling change in composition that student writers sometimes refer to it as "instant style." It can add new interest, new tone, and new and unexpected grace to even the most pedestrian piece of writing.

Unfortunately, a great many students never master parallelism simply because they are scared off by the definition. It's a definition cast in grammatical terms because it deals with a grammatical structure. If you are a grammar-shy student, you are likely to take one look at it and fall into a faint.

The irony of this is that the definition of parallel structure is actually a good deal harder to understand than is parallel structure itself. The sensible thing to do, therefore, is to ignore the definition for the time being and to learn parallel structure the way you learned to talk—by listening to it.

Look for the Common Denominator

Parallelisms range all the way from the very simple to the extremely complex, but they all have one thing in common.

147

You should have little difficulty finding this common denominator in the following examples:

> 1. He was the kind of man who knew what he wanted, who intended to get it, and who allowed nothing to stand in his way.

> 2. She wanted to walk out, to get in the car and drive forever, to leave and never come back.

> 3. They went to London, to Paris, to Rome.

> 4. He felt that Mary had changed, that she had moved into another world, that she had left him behind.

> 5. If we are to survive, if we are to have even the hope of surviving, we must end the nuclear race.

> 6. To know you are right is one thing; to prove it, quite another.

The common denominator, of course, is the repetition of some element in the sentence. It is *not,* you will notice, the repetition of an idea. A parallelism does not say the same thing in different words. The repetition is a repetition of *structure.*

Look at Sentence 1. In this, the *who* clause is repeated: "the man *who knew . . . , who intended . . . ,* and *who allowed . . .*" Each clause makes a separate point, but each has the same structure.

In Sentence 2, the infinitive phrase is repeated: *to walk, to get, to leave.*

In Sentence 3, it's the prepositional phrase: *to London, to Paris, to Rome.*.

In Sentence 4, it's the *that* clause (commonly called a noun clause): "*that Mary had changed, that she had moved . . . ,* that she had left . . ." Notice that the tense of the verb remains the same, although the verb itself changes.

In Sentence 5, the repetition is an *if* clause. This is an economical method, by the way, of setting up all the *if*'s in any kind of proposition—rather a handy thing to have around if you are working with an "iffy" sort of thesis, particularly as you sum up an argument: "If, then, such-and-such is true, if so-and-so is right, if the situation is thus, then . . ." The repeated structure lends grace to logic, and the sentence resolves itself into a triumphant final flourish.

The last one, Sentence 6, is an example of a "balanced sentence." The infinitives *to know* and *to prove* are parallel, and the two clauses are balanced on either side of a semicolon. Since both clauses deal with the same idea (rightness), it is not necessary to repeat the first clause in its entirety. In fact, the abruptness of the second clause adds emphasis.

Balance, of course, is always inherent in parallelism. Various parts of the sentence balance themselves against each other, weight for weight. Phrase balances with phrase, clause with clause, idea with idea, thus creating a strong and satisfying sense of interior wholeness in a sentence.

The foregoing examples represent only a fraction of the parallels possible with the English language. The more you practice, the more ways you will discover. You can, for example, use a double parallel:

> If we are to survive, if we are to have even the hope
> of surviving, we must end the nuclear race, and we
> must end it soon.

Or you can place whole sentences in parallel position, even whole paragraphs. You can use parallels within parallels, in patterns of increasing intricacy. The main thing is to begin.

ASSIGNMENT

1. Complete this unfinished sentence with a series of *who* clauses: "He always made trouble. He was the kind of boy who . . ."
2. Complete the following sentence with a series of infinitive phrases: "To be successful, she thought, she needed only to . . ."
3. Using *to* as your preposition, complete this sentence with a series of prepositional phrases: "In desperate search for a cure, he went to . . ."
4. Using *of* as your preposition, complete this sentence with

a series of prepositional phrases: "She was afraid of everything: of . . ."

5. Complete this sentence with a series of *that* clauses: "He complained that the children made too much noise, that . . ."
6. Write a sentence beginning with three *if* clauses.
7. Write a sentence ending with three *if* clauses.
8. Complete this sentence by interrupting it with two parallel *if* clauses: "The problem of race relations, if . . . , and if . . . , must be solved."
9. Write a balanced sentence modeled on Sentence 6 on page 148 but using different infinitives.
10. Write a sentence that contains a double parallel.

The Smaller Parallels

The parallels you have studied so far have been stylistic, or literary, and therefore relatively sophisticated. In effect you have started your study of parallels at the top, on the theory that this provides the best possible vantage point for watching operations at ground level—the small, simple parallels used every day in all kinds of writing.

These smaller parallels are exceedingly important, for any big, swooping parallel needs, like a bridge, solid support on the ground.

Whenever a sentence contains two or more similar elements, these elements must be kept parallel, no matter how small they are. In a series of nouns, for example, each item must be a noun; in a series of adjectives, each item must be an adjective; and so forth:

Nouns:
> *Not:* She liked ball games, hikes, and going to picnics.
> *But:* She liked ball games, hikes, and *picnics*.

That *going to* in the first example throws the whole parallel out of kilter. It's the kind of awkwardness that hits a reader's ear like the squawk of an unoiled hinge. Watch out for similar jarring notes in the following:

Adjectives:

> *Not:* He was lazy, good-humored, likeable, and sort of a crook.
> *But:* He was lazy, good-humored, likeable, and *slightly crooked.*

Adverbs:

> *Not:* She walked steadily and in a big hurry.
> *But:* She walked steadily and *swiftly.*

Verbs:

> *Not:* She combed her hair, put on her coat, and her purse was checked.
> *But:* She combed her hair, put on her coat, and *checked her purse.*

Suppose you are one of those students so impervious to grammar that you can't tell an adverb from an aardvark. You can still keep your parallels lined up. Use your ear and your common sense. You can tell whether words need to be alike or not. Take it from there.

The same principle operates in relation to pairs. Pairs are usually balanced on either side of *and, but,* and *or.* Keep them equal, as shown in the corrections below:

> *Not:* She was an expert driver and could also repair cars.
> *But:* She was an expert driver and *mechanic.*

> *Not:* He was intelligent but a boring boy.
> *But:* He was intelligent but *boring.*
>
> or
>
> He was *a brain* but *a bore.*

> *Not:* Her ambition was to act in movies and playing certain roles.
> *But:* Her ambition was to act in movies and *to play* certain roles.

> *Not:* He wanted either money or to be famous.
> *But:* He wanted either money or *fame.*

151

It's always a good idea to take a sharp look at what you use with connectives (like *and, but,* and *as well as*), particularly at the tail end of a sentence. That's where the slippage is likely to occur:

Not: The trip into town had been both difficult and a great expense.

But: The trip into town had been both difficult and *expensive.*

Not: He wanted to pour all his effort into the job, to do it well, but keeping the time down as much as possible.

But: . . . to do it well, but *to do it quickly.*

Not: He worked hard to maintain his high grades, but he yearned for popularity as well as being recognized as a good student.

But: . . . for popularity as well as *academic success.*

Some of the trickiest parallels to control are those using *either . . . or, neither . . . nor, not only . . . but also,* and *first/second/third.* The first two pairs, particularly, are tricky:

Not: Either I'm always in debt or in trouble.

But: Either I'm always in debt or I'm always in trouble.

or

I'm always either in debt or in trouble.

Not: He is the kind of dog that will neither mind his mistress nor his master.

But: He is the kind of dog that will mind neither his mistress nor his master.

The easiest way to check these two for proper position is to call a halt, mentally, immediately after *either* or *neither* and check the weight on both sides of *or* or *nor:*

| I'm always either | in debt | or | in trouble. |
| She could be neither | kind | nor | cruel. |

The weight must be the same on both sides. Word balances word, phrase balances phrase. The same principle governs *not only . . . but also:*

| That will scare not only | Sally | but also | the cat. |

That will scare not only   Sally but also the cat.
They hoped to go not only to London but also to Paris.

The problem with *first/second/third* is that one item can easily slip out of line:

> First, the photography is poor; second, the sound track is below average; third, I don't think it's in very good taste.

That last item is, of course, out of parallel; write "third, the whole thing is in poor taste," and it falls into line.

The first item in any series sets the pattern, and all other items must conform to it. The first item in the following example is a *that* clause; therefore, *that* must be repeated after *second* and *third:*

> After he entered college he realized clearly, first, that he should have worked harder in high school; second, that he would have to work hard now to keep up; and third, that he could succeed only by learning self-discipline.

Compare this example with Sentence 4 on page 148. Structurally they are exactly the same. The only difference is that here the clauses are numbered. (The structure is brought to your attention again because you may get so involved with numbering that you forget about keeping the items parallel.)

The smallest of all the parallels has been kept until last—the use of articles (*a, an, the*) and prepositions (*to, by, for, from,* and so on) in a series. The rule: *If you repeat an article or a preposition once, repeat it every time—or not at all.* For example:

> A house, a yard, a garden, and a pool.
> or
> A house, yard, garden, and pool.

> For love, for honor, for fame, or for money.
> or
> For love, honor, fame, or money.

Summary

Some parallels are a matter of simple logic. Controlling them is mainly a housekeeping chore, a necessary straightening and tidying-up that every writer learns to do as a matter of course. The subtler and more complex parallels are the real challenge and the true delight of writing. Requiring the most artful balance of many elements, parallels are exciting things to handle. Even more exciting, however, is the immediate and startling improvement they can make in your writing style.

Parallelism on any level is simply, in the final analysis, control. Keep all elements of equal value parallel, whether they are big elements or small, and your sentences can't straggle off raggedly this way and that. They will have the sense of wholeness, balance, and architectural soundness that pleases the ear and satisfies the mind.

ASSIGNMENT

1. Each of the sentences below contains some kind of faulty parallelism. Rewrite each sentence correctly.

    a. She planned a trip to the country, a visit with her grandmother, and taking long hikes with her cousin.
    b. The old man was gentle, kind, and gave away a lot of money to the poor.
    c. She put the model airplane together neatly, accurately, and with a great deal of skill.
    d. The girl wiped the windshield, cleaned off the dirty headlights, polished the chrome trim, and even the hubcaps were checked.
    e. He hoped either to be elected president of his class or make the highest grades.
    f. She was intelligent as well as having a lot of friends.
    g. He had to have the suit both altered and to have it cleaned.
    h. The thing she most looked forward to was a hot meal and having a hot bath.
    i. He enjoyed going to the movies as well as trips to the theater.
    j. Either the boys disliked or ignored him.

k. Their purpose was not only to take special courses in science but in art.

l. The committee is not only working hard to preserve historical landmarks but is also interested in developing a local museum.

m. They believe that a museum will promote greater interest in local history, that it will enrich the lives of school children in the community, and will become a major tourist attraction.

n. Many students believe that to be popular is happiness.

o. Study develops the mind, exercise develops the body, and understanding is developed by experience.

p. She made it clear, first, that she had no faith in the project; second, that she would not support it; and that, third, she would advise her friends against it.

q. They arrived in town by bus, by train, by plane, and even walking.

2. President John F. Kennedy's inaugural address contained a number of striking parallelisms. Find at least five in the selections from the address, below. Copy them exactly.

We observe today not a victory of party but a celebration of freedom, symbolizing an end as well as a beginning, signifying renewal as well as change. . . .

. . . Let the word go forth from this time and place, to friend and foe alike, that the torch has been passed to a new generation of Americans, born in this century, tempered by war, disciplined by a hard and bitter peace, proud of our ancient heritage, and unwilling to witness or permit the slow undoing of those human rights to which this nation has always been committed, and to which we are committed today at home and around the world.

So let us begin anew, remembering on both sides that civility is not a sign of weakness, and that sincerity is always subject to proof. Let us never negotiate out of fear, but let us never fear to negotiate.

Now the trumpet summons us again—not as a call to bear arms, though arms we need; not as a call to battle, though embattled we are; but a call to bear the burden of a long twilight struggle, year in and year out, "rejoicing in hope, patient in tribulation," a struggle against the common enemies of man: tyranny, poverty, disease, and war itself.

And so, my fellow Americans, ask not what your country can do for you; ask what you can do for your country.

3. Below is a description of an animal lab. Choose a subject of your own—perhaps a library, a dormitory, a restaurant, any place you have observed closely—and write a description that imitates the passage below. Match its sentence structure, parallels, figures of speech, and so forth, with suitable constructions of your own.

> The animal lab is full of strange, muted sounds. Somewhere down the hall, behind closed doors, monkeys gossip incessantly, their voices thin, bored, faintly exasperated, like the voices of office workers on an endless coffee break. Now and then a lemur's cry— high, sweet, full of grief and hope—breaks through the monkeys' mindless chatter. And something else whispers in the air, a small rustling and scuttling sound, anciently familiar and vaguely disquieting: rats are nearby.
>
> They are, in fact, nearby in great numbers, in the big colony room. These are elegant rats, refined rats, plump and docile and immaculate, white of fur and innocently pink of claw and tail. Science has bred out of them nearly every resemblance to their ugly ancestors. These placid aristocrats have never seen a ship's hold, or a garbage dump, or a littered alley; they have never run from snapping dogs nor crept at night through secret tunnels in the walls of decayed tenements. But they still make, in their clean wire cages, the ageless sound that rats in movement have always made.

VOCABULARY

1. Define the following words:

disquieting	incessantly	pedestrian
docile	inherent	placid
immaculate	intricacy	scuttling
impervious	lemur	vantage

156

2. Choose the word from the above list that most nearly fits the meaning of each sentence below:

    a. The pattern in the lace was extremely delicate and complex, a web of leaves and flowers interwoven with gold thread.

    b. An iron-willed leader, she could not be reached by any appeal to her emotions.

    c. From the attic window they had a splendid view of everything that went on in the street.

    d. Every word, every gesture suggested a strong instinct for drama.

    e. He was quiet, submissive, and willing to learn.

    f. Her writing style is quite ordinary.

    g. His white shirt was spotlessly clean.

    h. She refused to believe the rumor, but it made her uneasy.

3. Using all the words in the vocabulary list above, write six sentences, each containing one of the parallelisms illustrated in Examples 1–6 on page 148.

11

A Way with Words

You have spent a great deal of time learning some rather difficult techniques of style. Now it behooves you to see to it that you have a vocabulary worthy of those techniques.

Don't expect to write well with a vocabulary limited to the perfectly familiar—and therefore perfectly easy—words you already know. It can't be done, and the sooner you face that fact, the faster your progress will be. Other things being equal, the bigger your vocabulary, the better your writing. It's a matter of simple arithmetic. The more words you know, the more choices you can make; and the more choices you can make, the better chance you have of finding the exact word you need at any given time—what the French call *le mot juste,* the word that fits precisely the thought you want to express.

You have been working regularly with vocabulary assignments, but you should begin now, if you have not already done so, to intensify your efforts to improve and enlarge your word supply. Don't waste your time envying the lucky few who, through wide reading or constant association with unusually fluent people, already have large vocabularies.

Yours can be just as large, or larger. Don't try to find excuses for a poor vocabulary ("I'm too dumb. I'm too busy. I've got other things on my mind."). A poor vocabulary can't be excused—not in this day and age. It can only be explained. And the explanation can be summed up in one word: *laziness.* If you want a good vocabulary, you can have it. But don't expect it to come to you without effort; you've got to go after it.

Go after it first in a big general way: by reading. Read for pleasure. Read everything you can find on any subject that interests you. Read short stories, novels, articles. Read the newspaper. Read matchbook covers. Read everything. Soak up words wherever you find them. The more you read, the more words you will know.

When you find a word you don't know, *look it up.* You've probably heard that so many times during your school career that it no longer registers. Make it register. Look it up. Take a fresh look at those words. They mean something. Get a pocket dictionary and park it in your hip pocket or your bag so that it's always handy, and *use* it. Underline new words and list them separately on your own private word list. Don't try to persuade yourself that you'll remember a new word just because you looked it up. You won't. Write it down. Install an imaginary red light in your brain that says, "Stop! Look it up! List it!" every time you see or hear an unfamiliar word.

As soon as you have a new word nailed down in your mind, use it in conversation. Make a game of it, not a classroom exercise. Try at least one new word a day, and pick an audience that you aren't afraid of—your little sister or your barber or even your dog. Get used to the new word in your mouth. You'll be surprised at how quickly it loses its strangeness. Tell your prattling little sister that she's *loquacious,* tell the barber you want an *orthodox* haircut, tell Rover he's entirely too *obstreperous.* In no time at all, the new words will have moved comfortably into position as part of your working vocabulary.

Then if your new words are met with surprise by your

enemies, who sometimes have the annoying habit of dropping their jaws and saying, "Wozzat mean? Watcha talkin' about?" you can have the exquisite pleasure of replying, "Don't be *obtuse*, Charlie." (It isn't wise to do this, of course, if you think Charlie might look up *obtuse*, particularly if he is bigger than you are and given to violence.)

Synonyms and Antonyms

In addition to a dictionary, you need one other tool for improving your vocabulary: Roget's (pronounced roh-ZHAYZ) *Thesaurus,* a remarkable little book that could well prove to be the most valuable tool of all. Completely indexed for easy reference, it lists synonyms and antonyms for hundreds of common words. But it goes beyond this. Look up a word for almost any idea you want to express and you will find not only all the other words that mean the same thing but also all sorts of related words and phrases, the kind that tease at the edges of your mind but that you can never quite pin down. You know what you want to say, but you can't quite say it? Look in Roget.

Roget's *Thesaurus* is not a dictionary. It gives no definitions. But you will almost invariably find exactly the word you want. A word may be followed by a dozen synonyms, or more, but suddenly you see one of them and think, "That's it." It locks instantly into place in your mind, wonderfully and exactly right, the very word you were looking for.

Here, for example, are just a few of the words Roget lists in connection with the single verb *inquire:*

> seek, look for, reconnoiter, explore, rummage, ransack, pry, peer, pursue, scrutinize, ferret out, unearth, agitate, investigate, analyze, anatomize, dissect, sift, winnow

These, remember, are just a *few* of those listed in the entry. If you want to know the others, get a copy of Roget and rummage through it. Ransack those lists. Ferret out the word you need.

160

One of the most satisfying things about a thesaurus is that it often supplies a choice where you think no choice exists. No doubt you have had the experience of writing a paper in which one word crops up insistently again and again. It begins to sound repetitious and dull, and you know it, but no matter how you cudgel your brains, you can't think of anything to put in its place. This is where Roget comes to the rescue. If the word has a substitute, a thesaurus will have it. And even if no substitute exists, a thesaurus will probably give you hints for rephrasing an idea or shifting an emphasis, thus neatly solving the problem by avoiding it.

Best of all, Roget makes you aware as never before of the tremendous selection of words available to express every shade of meaning, all of them clustered around one word for easy picking and so cross-referenced that if you can't find what you want in one place, you are directed elsewhere. You may not always know the meaning of every word given, but that's what the dictionary is for.

If, for example, you want to describe Charlie, that obnoxious fellow, you have the happy opportunity to choose from *abhorrent, despicable, odious, abominable, repulsive, malicious, rancorous, churlish, surly, invidious, venomous, hostile,* and *repulsive*—and that's just a beginning. Pick a good one and check it out with the dictionary, just to be sure you have the exact shade of meaning you want. The dictionary not only points out subtle differences in meaning but often supplies examples that help still further in making close distinctions. You will want to do your best by Charlie.

Nearly every classroom has a king-size dictionary, and many English classrooms have Roget's *Thesaurus* or a similar book of synonyms. But these are for classroom use. You should have a small pocket edition of each that you can call your own. Put your name on them. Use them constantly. Guard them. The world is full of pocket-book snatchers. Snarl menacingly at borrowers. When you have finally finished your formal education, nothing—not even a crisp new diploma—will be a prouder badge of distinction than these two books, tattered, dog-eared, worn out from use.

Big Words and Small

A good writing vocabulary needs to be big, but that does not mean it should be made up exclusively of big words. Most particularly, it does not mean a vocabulary in which big words or whole phrases are substituted for perfectly adequate small words. Any writer who insists on using polysyllabic words like *accompanied* instead of *went with, at that point in time* instead of *then,* merely succeeds in sounding like a stuffed shirt.

Generally speaking, when you can choose between an easy, familiar expression and one that seems more "dignified," the easier word is the better choice *if it means exactly the same thing.* The more formal expression may be used occasionally, simply for the sake of variety, but consistent formality will make your writing sound impossibly prim and genteel. Some other high-flown substitutes that crop up all too often in bad writing are these:

appeared to be	(seemed)	manner	(way)
consumed	(ate)	obtained	(got)
desired	(wanted)	possessed	(had)
implemented	(followed up)	received	(got)
individual	(he, she, person, woman, man, etc.)	required	(needed)
		securing	(getting)
informed	(told)	similar to	(like)
		stated	(said)

No hard-and-fast rule can be laid down against using any of these expressions, since you may on occasion use any one of them without ill effect. But give them as wide a berth as possible. The best way to guard yourself against their use is to avoid the temptation of trying to sound dignified. Your writing will have natural dignity if it is a serious and thoughtful presentation of your ideas. The moment you try to doctor it up with high-flown, stately sounding polysyllabic substitutes for direct and simple words, you become the victim of creeping pomposity.

Always be suspicious of any impulse on your part to impress a reader with your dignity. No reader was ever warmed by a blast of hot air. The thing to look for, always, is *le mot juste*—not the pompous substitute-word that trumpets what a smart person you are, but the precisely chosen word that instantly transmits an exact shade of meaning.

Don't make the mistake, however, of depending always upon the short or familiar words. Some of these words are so familiar that they no longer have any specific meaning. This is particularly true of descriptive words like *good, nice, pretty, ugly, bad, awful, terrific, neat, dumb, funny, crazy, great, fine*—and a host of others that you recognize instantly as the currency of everyday speech. They are appallingly inadequate in writing, and these words, above all others, should be traced through Roget and the dictionary until you find a more precise meaning for your particular purpose. Just to get an idea of the immense choice available, look at some of the possible substitutes available for the word *crazy:*

> insane, mad, lunatic, unhinged, unbalanced, psychopathic, cracked, *non compos mentis,* touched, bereft of reason, moonstruck, scatterbrained, maniacal, delirious, irrational, lightheaded, incoherent, rambling, doting, wandering, amuck, frantic, raving, pixilated, eccentric, demented, deranged, schizophrenic

Or examine the shades of bigness in these substitutes for *big:*

> bulky, huge, mountainous, enormous, massive, impressive, important, weighty, considerable, vast, immense, stupendous, mighty, monstrous, titanic, gigantic, colossal, gargantuan, voluminous, mammoth, corpulent, burly, portly, elephantine

With such a wealth of words to choose from, poverty of expression is inexcusable. If you dwell in the slums of language, if you refuse to claim your inheritance, you have no one to blame but yourself. English is the richest language in the world, and for hundreds of years people have worked lovingly and patiently to gather it together in dictionary and thesaurus—to explain it and classify it for your convenience—so that you can pick and choose exactly what you want from it for the rest of your life. It is all freely yours for the taking. You can be a prince or a pauper, depending upon how much of your inheritance you choose to claim.

It's up to you.

The Solemn Vapors

Almost every student comes down once in a while with a bad case of abstractionitis, or Solemn Vapors, a writer's disease associated with excessive use of big, general words like *equality, justice, patriotism, democracy, morality, idealism, happiness.* These are important and necessary words, and it would be impossible for us to get along without them, but they are a special hazard in writing because they tempt writers into believing they have said something profound when they may have actually said almost nothing—at least nothing that a reader can take hold of in any real way.

An abstraction is any word that applies to a large class of things rather than to any single, concrete object or idea. Every word is in some measure an abstraction, but some abstractions are more general than others. *Structure,* for example, is more general than *house, house* is more general than *hovel,* and *hovel* is more general than *a miserable little shack with broken windows and a sagging door.* The more general the meaning of a word, the more abstract it is likely to be.

Too many abstract words make for vagueness, even meaninglessness. Good writing is specific; it makes things real. Observe that as you move away from abstraction toward something more specific—from *structure* to *miserable shack*—you create a sharper mental image and therefore a stronger sense of reality. You can never get away from abstractions entirely, but you should try constantly to pin them down, embody them in things that are real and tangible.

The opposite of *abstract* is *concrete.* Concrete words are words that stand for real things, things that appeal in one way or another to the senses. Unlike an abstraction, which exists only as a rather hazy mental concept, a concrete word is something you can see or hear or smell or taste or touch. And it is concrete words that give your writing color and texture and the solid feeling of realness.

Stick to concrete words as much as possible. If you are writing an essay on an abstract subject, pin it down quickly with specific examples that illustrate exactly what you mean. Don't float off on a cloud of vague and virtuous general terms.

Perhaps the best way to demonstrate the difference between concrete and abstract language is by a single example with which you are undoubtedly already familiar, a phrase that has become a classic example of the power in a concrete image as opposed to an abstraction. The phrase swept the country, instantly becoming a byword, simply because it translated an abstract idea into a vivid, immediately understood, specific image:

> Happiness is a warm puppy.

The abstractionist would have written:

> One characteristic of the condition of happiness is a quality of contentment or pleasure associated with complete physical comfort, satisfaction with a given environment, and a sense of being loved.

The warm puppy is now such a cliché that no writer over the age of eleven would dream of using it (except perhaps satirically), but even the most rigorous antisentimentalist would admit that the warm puppy says a great deal more than the abstraction.

Symptoms of the Solemn Vapors often include misty eyes, outthrust jaw, a tendency to clench the fists, and a warm feeling of self-righteousness in the area of the breastbone. If you feel an attack coming on, cold baths may help, but for best results go back to Chapter 6 for a quick review of the picture-frame paragraph. That should help you keep in touch with the things of this world.

Metaphor and Simile

One effective way to make an abstraction concrete is by metaphor—a single vivid image that illustrates an idea. That warm puppy, for example, is a metaphor—an instantaneous representation of happiness that is a hundred times more vivid and meaningful than a dozen paragraphs of description or explanation. *A metaphor never explains; it creates an image, and the image* shows *what it means.*

Oddly, the more vivid and apt a metaphor is, the more likely it is to turn into a cliché. Everybody likes it, and everybody uses it; and as a result, it becomes so much a part of everyday speech that it loses all its original force and color. "Hitch your wagon to a star," for example, must have been a startlingly vivid figure of speech when it was first coined, but the picture has been rubbed out of it by universal use. As in "All that glitters is not gold" or "Birds of a feather flock together," the vividness has become triteness, and no self-respecting author uses such phrases except as brief allusions or after giving them playful new twists: "All that gold was not just glitter"; "birds of a very different feather"; "an actress whose stardom is hitched to a wagon train."

A simile is a slowed-down metaphor; instead of jumping straight to its image, it arrives by way of an *as* or *as if* or *like.* The same kind of wear and tear that renders metaphors impotent also affects similes. Typical worn-out similes are "hungry as a bear," "quick as a wink," "old as the hills," "feel like a million." Avoid these expressions entirely (in speaking as well as in writing if possible).

A good metaphor becomes a commonplace precisely because it expresses an idea so well. The writer, however, whose whole purpose is to say things well, can't use commonplaces. This is one of the great ironies of writing. Only new images, new metaphors, fresh ways of expressing ideas will satisfy readers. For this, a writer must fall back upon personal experience and imagination, must learn (and this is the whole secret of metaphor) to describe one thing by comparing it directly or indirectly to another:

> She pushed herself down the street slowly, patiently, like an indomitable old turtle, her immense body balanced precariously on stumpy legs, her small head retracted into the folds of her collar, only the curved beak of her nose protruding into the bitter air. The buckles of her flapping galoshes made a sound like the clatter of ancient claws.

Note that this metaphor is extended; each detail of the old woman's appearance relates one way or another to the turtle image—*immense body, stumpy legs, small head, retracted, curved beak, ancient claws.* In an extended metaphor, details must be kept consistent with the original image.

It is not necessary, however, to extend a metaphor to this length. One sentence can provide a single image before you move on to fulfill some other purpose in a paragraph. Note, in the examples below, how the metaphor or the simile is sometimes carried by a verb, sometimes by a noun or an adjective, sometimes by a combination of elements:

> eyes as hard and wise and wary as an old turtle's
>
> a jungle of ropes and pulleys and discarded scenery
>
> his voice cut through her thoughts like a rusty saw
>
> a pasted-on smile
>
> sausage-fingered
>
> the craggy landscape of his face
>
> music pulling at her feet

The principle for both metaphor and simile is the same: *Both of them make or imply a comparison between two things; one of the two things compared is literal, the other figurative.* A purely literal comparison—"She looks like her mother"—is not metaphorical. She quite literally does look like her mother. But "She looks like a thundercloud" is metaphorical. Nobody really looks like a thundercloud. The connotation, however, is clear.

It is possible, of course, to use too many metaphors and similes in your writing. When this happens, the writing lacks some necessary hard edge of reality—it "goes soft." Nobody can tell you how much metaphor is too much, but you should be suspicious of your writing if it takes on a consistently dreamy, hazy quality that sounds pretty but never makes its point sharply and directly. Fortunately, the cure is not difficult. You need only train yourself to alternate metaphorical expression with abrupt, unadorned, precise statement. If you are naturally adept at metaphor, you probably have an ear that is naturally well tuned to language, and you will quickly appreciate the improvement in your style when you make it a little harder and more vigorous.

Most students, however, use far too little figurative language. You should experiment with it often, for it can give your writing greater excitement, a more interesting texture. Metaphors are usually more subtle than similes, and frequently more brilliant, but here again variety is the key. Use both—and every variety of both. It would probably be wise to hold similes down to one per paragraph; *like* and *as* and *as if* have a way of sticking out too obviously when they become too numerous. But let yourself go with all other kinds of metaphor. A good paragraph can probably support as many of them as you can dream up.

Allusion

Allusion is indirect reference, and it is simply another way to strike a responsive chord in a reader. Familiar allusions are easiest. "He has a Madison Avenue mentality," "Even the local Scrooge was there," "She was the neighborhood Pollyanna," "They loathed the office Casanovas."

Never explain an allusion. If the reader understands it, this sudden and unexpected thrust of the familiar is a pleasant surprise. If the reader doesn't understand it, no harm done. The meaning of the sentence is still quite clear.

Allusions can range from the familiar to the highly literary, with stops in between for commonly recognized literary forms like children's verse and stories:

> He was able to stay on his Jack Sprat diet only one
> week.

> She could play fairly well, but she was no Pied Piper.
>
> She had no taste for the role of cat looking at king.

Any familiar literary reference can be used allusively, either seriously or ironically:

> This brave new world requires brave new people.
>
> I was not yet one-and-twenty, but I was full of rue.
>
> He sat at the door like Cerberus.
>
> Having accomplished nothing, they folded their tents and stole sheepishly away.
>
> How do I hate algebra? Let me count the ways.

The wider your knowledge of literature, the richer your sources of allusion. Literary allusions are a particular source of pleasure for the discriminating reader, for they reveal in the subtlest possible way that writer and reader share a common literary heritage. Unlike direct, factual quotations requiring extra typographical details, the allusion is deftly woven into context, and from there it sends its special signal to any reader equipped to receive it.

Summary

Increase your vocabulary consciously by reading, by using your thesaurus and your dictionary, by practicing new words in speech and writing until they become a natural and familiar part of your thinking process. To enrich your vocabulary is to enrich not only your writing but your life, for the more words you know, the better you can understand and interpret your own experience.

Make abstractions real by using your senses. Translate big, vague terms into the tangible objects of real life. Make yourself *see* what you write about: Give your ideas substance with specific details, with real things that have color and shape, things that can be touched or tasted or smelled or heard. Strive always toward realness.

For this realness use metaphor and simile. *Show* what you mean, in images. And use allusion to maintain the sense of friendly communication, of shared experience, with your reader. Connect, relate, compare—and thus delight.

QUESTIONS

1. What is *le mot juste?*
2. What should you do every time you come across a word that is new to you?
3. What is a synonym?
4. What is an antonym?
5. Describe Roget's *Thesaurus.* What was the original meaning of the word *thesaurus?*
6. Will your writing have more dignity if you make a point of using big words in place of smaller, more familiar words? Explain your answer.
7. Explain the meaning of this statement about vocabulary: "You can be a prince or a pauper, depending upon how much of your inheritance you choose to claim."
8. What does the author mean by the phrase "the slums of language"?
9. What are the Solemn Vapors?
10. What is the difference between an abstract word and a concrete word? Give at least two examples not used in the text.
11. What is the difference between a metaphor and a simile? Give examples.
12. What is an allusion?

ASSIGNMENT

1. Write a brief essay defending the idea that a student's personal copies of a pocket dictionary and a thesaurus, worn out from use, may be better evidence of a good education than a diploma.
2. Rewrite each of the following sentences so that it express-es the same idea in concrete rather than abstract terms. (For example, "Vigorous physical exercise before

breakfast is an excellent way to start the day" can be made concrete by saying "A few push-ups before breakfast can start the day right.")

    a. She was tired of domestic chores.
    b. The available reading material was very scanty.
    c. Certain physical characteristics gave evidence of his anger.
    d. Real elegance, to her, was jewelry.
    e. The daily consumption of some kind of fresh fruit is helpful in reducing the need for medical attention.
    f. He longed for contact with nature.
    g. His clothing was obviously old and worn.
    h. He was tired of the pressures of city life.
    i. He would have given a great deal for some kind of solid nourishment.
    j. What he needs is some kind of strong disciplinary treatment.

3. Choose one of the sentences below as the first sentence of a descriptive paragraph. Use an extended metaphor to complete the description. (See the example on page 167.) Be sure to keep details consistent.

    a. She was as cool and assured as a duchess.
    b. He looked like a crafty, intelligent old goat.

4. Write five sentences in which you make some kind of familiar allusion. (See examples on page 169.) Be as original as possible.

5. Write five sentences in which you make a literary allusion. Your literature textbook may be helpful. Find a well-known quotation and work it into some meaning of your own. (See examples on page 169.)

VOCABULARY

1. Below is a list of words that are constantly overused. For each of the words, supply a list of at least ten other words that might be used in its place.

good	terrible	pretty	great
bad	wonderful	ugly	awful
big	happy	dull	mean
little	sad	exciting	nice

2. Use each of the words below in a periodic sentence that contains at least fifteen words.

behooves	invidious	obtuse
corpulent	loquacious	odious
demented	malicious	orthodox
eccentric	maniacal	surly
gargantuan	obstreperous	

12

Odds and Ends and Means

A multitude of small sins against style can plague writing. They are mostly sins of carelessness. Taken singly they may not seem to amount to much, but several of them added together can spoil a writer's whole effect. So, just as you take a final look in the mirror before appearing in public, you should take care of certain stylistic details before letting any piece of writing go out of your hands.

Collected for your examination on the following pages are many of the most common stylistic errors. It is not really possible to classify all of them in any kind of ascending (or descending) order according to offensiveness, but at least three deserve to be at the head of the list. The others are listed alphabetically for easy reference, but the Terrible Three come first. If you take any pride at all in your writing, you will not let any piece of it out of your hands until you have scrubbed out these abominations.

The Terrible Three

1. The *-wise* suffix: Some day the barbarians who started the fashion of adding *-wise* to the end of words will be

identified, run to earth, and suitably punished—preferably by being forced to spend the rest of their lives reading the compositions written by students who have followed in their footsteps. That would probably be best, justice-wise.

The use of -*wise* as a suffix has become so prevalent that no word in the language seems to be safe from it. In the course of an average day you are likely to hear that the cafeteria is serving some great desserts pie-wise; that someone is attractive clothes-wise, hair-wise, or face-wise; or that the weekend ahead looks pretty busy, study-wise.

It's enough to drive you crazy, style-wise.

Fortunately, the constant use of -*wise* is rapidly becoming a kind of national joke. In a few years it may be laughed out of existence. But it's a good idea to avoid it like poison. Meantime-wise, that is.

2. The *type* and *type of* habit: Throw these out along with -*wise*. It is particularly barbarous to use *type* as an adjective: "I have the type father who never loses his temper." Even with an *of* added ("I have the type of father who . . .") the expression is an assault on the ear of a discriminating reader.

Its use is bad partly because its meaning is nearly always subtly askew (usually the writer means *sort* or *kind* rather than *type),* but it is objectionable primarily because of its overuse. You can always change it for the better—usually by omitting it altogether. If you can't quite omit some needed shade of qualification that you think it adds, try one of the changes suggested below:

Not: I have the type of father who never loses his temper.
But: My father never loses his temper.

Not: She wasn't that type of girl.
But: She wasn't that kind of girl.

Not: She wore a Spanish-type costume.
But: She wore a Spanish costume.
    or
Her costume had a Spanish look.

Not: He was a Charles Chaplin-type actor.
But: His acting was Chaplinesque.
    or

174

Like Charles Chaplin, he . . .

Not: He used Hitler-type methods.
But: He used Hitlerian methods.
or
He used Hitler-like methods.

Not: They were best at guerrilla-type warfare.
But: They were best at guerrilla warfare.

3. *Manner* and *nature* phrases: *Manner* and *nature* are the pet words of the pompous, the long-winded, and the empty-headed. The two words are nearly always redundant. *In a polite manner* means "politely." *Comprehensive in nature* (or *of a comprehensive nature)* means "comprehensively."

To use *manner* and *nature* in phrases like those above is to indicate either that you are deliberately padding a sentence or that you have deluded yourself into thinking such phrases sound dignified. In either case, you annoy the reader.

All redundancies are annoying, *manner* and *nature* especially so because they seem to have a special aura of priggishness all their own. Put the words in dialogue and you can hear the priggishness:

"Do you like jazz?"
"I find it very exciting in nature."

And that should be enough to nip a beautiful friendship in the bud. (Of course, it could be worse. The response might have been, "I think that type playing is very exciting in nature, music-wise." But that's really too depressing to think about.)

Drop these stilted, unnecessary *manner* and *nature* phrases altogether. In fact, it might be a good idea to drop the words *manner* and *nature* altogether. Pretend they don't exist. You can get along without them perfectly well, and if they aren't in your vocabulary, you will never be tempted to use them in a phrase.

Drop all the Terrible Three. Put them behind you forever. Then you can devote your energies to locating and cleaning out the remaining abominations. They are listed below. Read them over carefully. Sensitize yourself to them. Become *aware.* That's half the battle.

The Troublesome Twenty-six

1. *as far as:* This phrase must be followed by *is concerned* or it is meaningless.

> *Not:* As far as studying, I've worked hard.
> *But:* As far as studying is concerned, I've worked hard.

2. *center around:* This is not possible. You can only center *on.*

3. *different:* Things are different *from* each other. Don't write *different than.* It makes no sense, just as it would make no sense to write "I want my books kept separate than the others." Different from, *from,* FROM.

4. *disinterested/uninterested:* The two words mean two different things, and the distinction is valuable. Preserve it. To be *disinterested* is to be impartial. If you are disinterested, you are interested but your emotions are not involved. If you take no interest, you are *uninterested.*

5. *due to:* Avoid this phrase altogether. It is graceless even when used correctly, and it is almost never used correctly.

6. *enthuse:* This word is reserved strictly for people who gush. Don't use it.

7. *fabulous, fantastic:* These two words have been so exhausted by overuse in daily speech and in advertising that they have become meaningless—and a sure sign of a limited vocabulary. Avoid them entirely unless you want your writing to sound like an ad for a Grade B movie or a month-end sale.

8. *feel bad:* If you are sick or unhappy, you feel *bad,* not *badly.*

9. *fewer/less: Fewer* refers to numbers, *less* to amounts. Don't use *less* in reference to anything you can count: *fewer students, less time, fewer problems, less trouble.*

10. *imply/infer:* To *imply* means "to suggest or indicate":

> Are you implying that he can't be trusted?
> *(Are you suggesting that . . . ?)*

To *infer* means "to draw a conclusion from":

> I didn't say that; you inferred it.
> *(That's what you drew from my statement.)*

11. indefinite pronouns *(each, everyone, everybody, either, neither, nobody):* All these pronouns are singular and must be treated consistently as singular. You wouldn't write "Everybody are taking their own lunch," so you shouldn't write "Everybody is taking their own lunch." *Their* is plural. The sentence should be, "Everybody is taking *his* or *her* own lunch."

Check out every indefinite pronoun by trying *he* or *she* in its place. If the rest of the sentence agrees with *he* or *she,* it will agree with the indefinite pronoun.

> Each of the girls wants her own way.
> *(Not: . . . their* own way.)

> Neither of the boys is capable of taking proper care of himself.
> *(Not: . . .* of *themselves.* And note the singular verb: Neither . . . *is.)*

If a sentence sounds too fussy and pedantic when you follow this rule for indefinite pronouns, recast the sentence. Don't break the rule; outwit it.

12. *irregardless:* This word is nonstandard English and is never to be used, regardless of how many times you hear it said by people who should know better. The word is *regardless.* The *ir-* is redundant; it means the same thing as the *-less* on the end of the word. Saying "irregardless" is rather like saying "irreckless" or "irruthless."

13. *like/as:* Don't use *like* when you mean *as* or *as if.* Here's an easy trick that will guarantee correct usage: Substitute *as though, as if, as,* or *in the way* wherever one of these will make sense in place of *like:*

> She acts like a queen.
> *(No substitute is possible here, so* like *is used correctly.)*

> She acts like she thinks she's a queen.
> *(A substitute would work here, so use it: She acts* as though *she thinks she's a queen.)*

> She acts like a queen would act.
> *(Use another substitute: She acts* in the way *a queen would act.)*

Never use *like* if one of the substitute phrases will work in its place. Test every *like* this way, and you can't be trapped into the wrong usage.

14. mixed metaphor: Don't mix one metaphor with another. The result may be unintentionally comic:

> He climbed the ladder of success across a sea of troubles, and left his footprint on the face of time.
> You've buttered your bread; now lie in it.

15. *off:* Always write *off;* never *off of.*

16. *perfect/unique:* If a thing is perfect, it's perfect. If it's unique, it's unique. It can't be *more perfect* (the Founding Fathers notwithstanding) or *more unique.* Perfection and uniqueness are absolute, therefore beyond comparison. Never use *more, most,* or *very* with either word.

17. *plus:* do not use *plus* in place of *and.* Don't say, "He was hungry, plus he was penniless." Save *plus* for problems in addition.

18. redundancies: Cut any word that repeats a meaning or pads a phrase without adding anything. Each of the italicized words or phrases below is redundant:

a distance of ten yards	*free* gift
advanced *forward*	*future* prospects
an *actual* fact	in addition, he *also*
another *one*	*past* history
at *the* present *time*	retreat *back*
equally as good as	small *in size*
false illusion	*usual* custom
few *in number*	

These are only a few of the redundancies that clutter English

usage. Look for others in your own writing, and avoid them.

19. *regarding:* This word is often misused:

> Regarding meals, the cafeteria will be open at noon.
> *(The cafeteria seems to be regarding the meals.)*

The easiest way to avoid this error is to avoid the word *regarding* altogether. Even correctly used, it tends to sound like committee language.

20. *similar to:* If you mean *like,* say *like.* Why beat around the bush?

21. slang: Using slang in writing is nearly always disastrous. Some students use it in the mistaken notion that it will make their writing sound informal. It won't. It will merely make it sound juvenile. Or "cute." Nothing is more repulsive in writing than cuteness.

22. *so:* Don't use *so* as a substitute for *very* or *terribly* or any other intensifier, as in "Exercise is so exhausting." You can get by with this in speech but not in writing. A reader expects a *so* in this position to be followed by *that:* "Exercise is so exhausting that . . ."

23. split infinitive: Don't put an adverb between the two parts of an infinitive: "to *really* think," "to *positively* believe," "to *suddenly* stop." Put the adverb before or after the infinitive. Better yet, leave it out altogether if you can do so without changing the meaning.

24. *the reason is:* Never say, "The reason is because . . ." And don't be fooled if other words come in between: "The reason for all these delays is because . . ." Instead, write:

> The reason is that . . .
> The reason for all these delays is that . . .

Or leave out the word *reason* and let *because* do the work:

> This happened. That happened. Because of these delays, . . .

25. trite expressions: Avoid the stale, ready-made expressions that have become overfamiliar and tiresome through constant use by second-rate speakers and third-rate writers. The following list of trite expressions is far from exhaustive, but it's representative:

acid test	green with envy
as luck would have it	last but not least
better late than never	Mother Nature
bitter end	needless to say
busy as a bee	rich and varied experience
depths of despair	ripe old age
easier said than done	sadder but wiser
festive occasion	slow but sure
few and far between	untold agony
finer things in life	words cannot express

26. *try:* Don't use *try and* when you mean *try to.* "I will try and be there" means that you are planning to do two things—you're going to try, and you're going to be there. You probably mean "I will try *to* be there."

Punctuation

Punctuation is not really a matter of style; it is a matter of necessity. Without it a writer's sentences would run together in one long toneless hum like this without any of the tones of speech for much of speech is made up of pauses of hesitations of small delays and full stops and it is punctuation that must supply writing with these small necessary silences without them it would take you twice as long to extract the meaning from anything you read and you would probably give up in anger or despair or else go quite mad from the din as your inner ear shrieked stop wait what was that you can see perhaps from this how difficult reading can be without punctuation.

In short, the only purpose of punctuation is to make reading easier.

Most punctuation indicates some kind of pause—the kind of pause you would use if you were speaking your sentences instead of writing them. A period, for example, indicates a full stop after a completed thought. The voice falls. The sentence is finished. That's it. Period.

Commas indicate the small pause *inside* the sentence. Listen to your sentences. A natural pause usually means that you need a comma:

> After all, nobody was to blame.
> *(Hear the pause after* all?)
>
> I'd love to go, but I really can't afford it.
> *(Hear the pause after* go?)
>
> He bought beans, potatoes, flour, and onions.
> *(Hear the pauses?)*
>
> He will also buy, if he is wise, a slab of bacon.
> *(Hear the pauses?)*

Failure to indicate pauses can lead to complete confusion. Look at the difference one small comma can make:

> Did the cat eat Mary?
> Did the cat eat, Mary?
>
> Percy, the cat has run away.
> Percy, the cat, has run away.

For every kind of pause natural to speech, written language has a corresponding mark of punctuation. Your ear alone can usually guide you to the proper use of periods and commas as they are demonstrated in the examples given here, but your ear is not enough to guide you in the use of all the markings.

Particularly the semicolon. Special attention must be called to it because many students seem to suffer from semicolonitis; semicolons tend to break out like measles all over their compositions. Apparently this is caused by a widespread belief that a semicolon is a kind of dignified comma. It is not. And it cannot be used in place of a comma. It's a kind of lightweight period, to be used only between closely related and evenly balanced complete thoughts.*

*The minor exceptions to this are of no consequence here.

Don't use it at random, tossing it into a pause just because you like the look of it. Honor the semicolon, and keep it wholly for the purpose that it was created to serve.

You should know, out of simple courtesy toward readers as well as respect for your own work, the proper use of all the other punctuation marks—colons, dashes, hyphens, apostrophes, parentheses, brackets, ellipses, quotation marks. All these are conventions, established by long usage to mean certain highly specific things.

Consult your grammar text. Learn all the fine distinctions. You will be surprised to find out how expressive a mere mark of the pen can be.

Summary

The transgressions listed in this chapter are not the only sins against style, but they are the most common—and the most likely to cause offense to the discriminating reader. The easiest way to handle them at first is to forget about them until you are ready to write the final draft of your paper. Then check. And check closely. Go through your entire paper, checking every sentence against every item on the list until you are certain you have rid yourself completely of all offenders.

It may be a slow, laborious process at first, and you will probably be appalled at how many items from the list show up in your writing. But gradually you will find that control has become automatic; you will find fewer and fewer of these barbarisms in your work because your heightened awareness of them will help you avoid them from the start. Habit will take over. The deliberate, painstaking, conscious hunting-down of stylistic faults leads eventually to a natural, almost unconscious avoidance of those faults.

The Terrible Three probably won't give you much trouble.

They are so laughably obvious, once you have become sensitized to them, that they are likely to disappear from your writing immediately. (They will also provide you with a fine source of private amusement as you discover how often *type of* and *-wise* and *manner* or *nature* turn up in the speech and writing of people who should know better.)

The remaining stylistic faults are a bit trickier and more persistent, but these too will eventually disappear as your awareness increases—as it will, if you are vigilant.

In any case, checking over your paper for the barbarisms listed in this chapter is a very slight effort indeed, compared with the effort you have already put into your essay. You have gone to the hard labor of creating something entirely new and entirely your own. Before you send it out to face the world, give it this final grooming. You owe that to yourself.

QUESTIONS

1. Notice the title of this chapter. What play on words do you find in it, and how does it relate to the content of this chapter?
2. What are the Terrible Three? Give an example of each.
3. Why is the phrase "center around" a logical impossibility?
4. Why is *fabulous* a poor word to use in most writing?
5. Logically, what is meant by "I feel badly"?
6. What is wrong with the word *irregardless?*
7. What test can you give the word *like* to make certain that you are using it correctly?
8. Why is it impossible to be "more perfect" or "more unique"?
9. What is a trite expression? Give examples other than those in the text.
10. Explain the real purpose of punctuation and give an illustration of its relation to sound.
11. What kind of pause does a comma indicate?
12. Explain the proper use of the semicolon.

1. Write three sentences using the suffix *-wise* as it should *not* be used. Then rewrite the sentence without the suffix. For example:

   > Everything was against him, percentage-wise.
   > All the percentages were against him.

2. Write three sentences using the expression "type" or "type of." Then rewrite correctly.

3. Write three sentences using the expressions "in nature," "of a . . . nature," and "in a . . . manner." Then rewrite correctly.

4. Write a sentence that demonstrates, in the same order listed in the chapter, each of the stylistic flaws in the Troublesome Twenty-six. Then after each sentence that contains a flaw, rewrite to get rid of the flaw. For example:

   > As far as exercise, few people get enough.
   > As far as exercise is concerned, few people get enough.

5. Find the stylistic flaw (or flaws) in each of the sentences below and rewrite the sentence correctly.

   a. Everybody who came to the meeting thought the discussion ought to center around their particular problem.
   b. Although he was not a doctor, he was very well informed as far as treatments for sore throat.
   c. The course was different than they expected.
   d. He acted like he was green with envy.
   e. Just to be sure of impartiality, get an uninterested judge for the contest.
   f. Regarding her future prospects, they look good.
   g. If he would get off of that subject, he could make a lot of forward progress.
   h. It was the most perfect kind of response to a silly question.
   i. Your letter seems to infer that you are ready to retreat back from your former position.

j. He felt badly about it, but it was all past history now, and outside of expressing his regrets he could do nothing but try and keep things under better control in the future ahead.

k. Each of the girls are asked to seriously consider the risks of the program.

l. She was too disinterested in the subject to attend the lecture, plus she was certain it would be similar to all the other lectures she had heard.

m. The movie was fabulous, but due to her job she had to leave before it ended.

n. He knew he might have false illusions about his ability, but he decided to enter the contest irregardless.

o. She found the hike so exhausting, and the reason was because she had slept for only a short period of time the night before.

6. On page 180, under Punctuation, is an entire paragraph that contains no punctuation after the first sentence. Beginning with the second sentence, copy the entire paragraph and punctuate it correctly.

13

Writing About Writing

The writing assignment that deals with some aspect of a work of literature is familiar to most students, and the range of subjects it covers is as broad as literature itself. You may be asked, for example, to interpret a poem, to analyze the role of a particular character in a work of fiction, to explain an author's point of view, or to make any number of other kinds of judgments about a given work. When you are asked to make a written judgment of this kind, you are being asked to write an essay.

For convenience, let's call such an essay the *literary paper*.

Like any essay, the literary paper is based upon a judgment—an opinion. You must, however, understand from the outset one very important thing about this particular kind of opinion: it has almost nothing to do with whether or not you "like" the literary work you are writing about. You are not being asked, when you are asked to write such a paper, to express your feelings about what you have read (feelings are not subject to debate). You are being asked to make a reasoned judgment that you can back up with *specific evidence* from the literary work you have read—poem, short story, novel, or some other form. Your approach, therefore, must be completely objective rather than emotional. That means you must ask questions that force you to think about the *meaning* of what you have read.

Let us say, for example, that you are studying Robert Frost's poem "Stopping by Woods on a Snowy Evening." On the surface, the poem looks very simple: a man stops his sleigh on a country road at dusk, gazes at the woods filling up with snow, and then goes on. But is that all there is to it? A man looking at a pretty scene? Surely the poem has more to it than this. So you ask questions. Why does he stop? What seems to hold him? Why does he finally go on? Why does Frost choose to end his poem by repeating the next to the last line? *What does it all add up to?* The moment you answer this question, you have the beginnings of an interpretation of the poem. You have an opinion on which to base an essay.

One very good way to start the process of forming an opinion is to ask yourself this question every time you come across anything in your reading that puzzles you: "What is the author trying to tell me here?" (Why does Hawthorne, in *The Scarlet Letter,* have Hester Prynne embroider the *A* on her clothing so richly that nobody could miss it? Why does the same author avoid telling the reader the name of the stranger in "The Ambitious Guest"? Why does William Golding allow Simon to be killed in *Lord of the Flies?* Why doesn't Shirley Jackson explain in "The Lottery" exactly where and when the lottery takes place?)

Why? That's the big question. Keep asking it. Your search for the answer will lead you to a better understanding of literature. Your new understanding of literature and your growing skill with the formal essay should enable you to master the literary paper very quickly.

The Thesis of the Literary Paper

The literary paper, like any essay, must have a thesis. The process for arriving at the thesis of the literary paper, however, is slightly different from the five-step procedure described in Chapter 2. Assuming that your teacher has given you a great deal of freedom in selecting a subject to write about, you have four steps to take:

1. Read the selection.

Obviously, you have to read the literary work in order to write about it intelligently. And you have to read it carefully and thoughtfully—every word. But before you even begin to read, ask yourself your first question: "In this book (let's say it is a book, *Grapes of Wrath,* for example) what is the author's (Steinbeck's) purpose?" Keep this question in mind all through your reading, because when you have finished, you will try to decide in your own mind whether the work is successful. This is a basic question to be asked about any literary work. What is the writer's purpose? The next questions stem from that: Does the writer succeed? *How* does the writer succeed?

As you read, notice what happens. To whom does it happen? Under what circumstances does it happen? Does anything or anyone change in any significant way in the course of the book? Why? How? What is the prevailing mood of the book (or poem or short story)? What is the tone?* Answers to questions like these will provide you with clues to the author's purpose and theme.

You will not read every literary selection in exactly the same way. The length of the selection will influence your reading of it. For example, it would take you hours to read *The Grapes of Wrath,* a novel, but you could read "The Ambitious Guest," a short story, in a half hour or less. And you could read the poem "Stopping by Woods on a Snowy Evening" in a minute or so.

Both the kind of selection you have chosen—novel, short story, poem—and the difficulty of the selection have a bearing upon the way you read. The short story and the novel can be approached much the same way, since both are fiction. The great difference is length (and therefore the extent to which the author can develop character and

---

*Tone refers to the writer's attitude toward his or her subject or to the attitude of the speaker in the selection. It is the emotional coloring the writer gives the work.

themes). You may have time to read the novel only once, coming back to parts of it for specific details as you develop your essay. You may have time to read a short story several times. And you may find it necessary to do so. Precisely because it is so brief and therefore so concentrated, the short story will often prove to be a more difficult subject than the novel.

The poem is something else, with problems all its own. Almost without fail, you can look at a poem and recognize it for what it is. You know it is a poem because it looks like a poem. In a general way, it has a familiar form. And that form, whatever it is, must be considered, for it supports and frames the rest of the poem.

Take as an example this poem by Archibald MacLeish:

Epistle to Be Left in the Earth

. . . It is colder now
                there are many stars
                           we are drifting
North by the Great Bear
                 the leaves are falling
The water is stone in the scooped rocks
                     to southward
Red sun gray air
           the crows are
Slow on their crooked wings
               the jays have left us
Long since we passed the flares of Orion
Each man believes in his heart he will die
Many have written last thoughts and last letters
None know if our deaths are now or forever
None know if this wandering earth will be found

We lie down and the snow covers our garments
I pray you
         you (if any open this writing)
Make in your mouths the words that were our names
I will tell you all we have learned
               I will tell you everything
The earth is round
          there are springs under the orchards

The loam cuts with a blunt knife
                                   beware of
Elms in thunder
                 the lights in the sky are stars
We think they do not see
                          we think also
The trees do not know nor the leaves of the grasses
                                              hear us
The birds too are ignorant
                            Do not listen
Do not stand at dark in the open windows
We before you have heard this
                               they are voices
They are not words at all but the wind rising
Also none among us has seen God
(. . . We have thought often
The flaws of sun in the late and driving weather
Pointed to one tree but it was not so)
As for the nights I warn you the nights are dangerous
The wind changes at night and the dreams come

It is very cold
                there are strange stars near Arcturus

Voices are crying an unknown name in the sky

You notice immediately as you glance at it that the poem
begins with three dots, or points of ellipsis. Something has
apparently happened before the poem opens, something you
don't know about yet. You notice also that the first short
lines are staggered downward and across the page, like
something falling and drifting away. This pattern continues
throughout the poem, which ends without punctuation of any
kind, suggesting that the aimless drifting is to continue,
perhaps forever.

The visual pattern of the poem reflects the action that
takes place in the poem itself: the earth has apparently
broken out of orbit and is drifting into space. The poem, of
course, expresses much more than this. It is, in fact a rather
chilling commentary about what life on this planet has
amounted to. But the point is that the form of a poem, and
even the arrangement of the lines on the page, can enhance

the ideas the poem conveys and add to the emotional impact upon the reader. Form is, therefore, a part of what the poem *is*.

As you begin to study a poem, ask yourself: "Is this a story? an observation? a picture? an impression? What goes on in it? Who is the speaker and what is he or she trying to say?" Read it aloud and listen for the sounds, but don't forget the sense. Look up any word or allusion that you don't understand. The key to the whole may be a very small part indeed.

Read, reread, and read again. And think, think, *think* about what you read. Overlook nothing. Ponder every phrase. That's the way to discover what a good poem is about and what a good poem is. If you find yourself committing certain lines to memory simply by puzzling over them so often, so much the better. The lines will stay with you a lifetime, a permanent source of pleasure.

To read the literary selection you are to write about is to take inventory. From your inventory will come the questions that lead to eventual understanding. And it is this inventory that will almost always supply you with all the evidence you need to support your thesis.

2. Make a list of controversial questions.

The questions you were asking yourself as you took inventory may not in every case be controversial. Some will have been purely factual. But when you begin to question attitudes, intentions, purposes, methods, and meanings, you are dealing with interpretation, that is, with opinions. And therein lies controversy.

Let's say you have chosen to write about some aspect of Mark Twain's *The Adventures of Huckleberry Finn*. One of the principal characters in the novel is Jim, a runaway slave. Suppose you ask yourself: "What was Mark Twain's attitude toward racial prejudice?" This is a question you could surely expect the book to answer, if only indirectly.

Or you may ask yourself: "Why does the ending of *Huckleberry Finn* seem so unlike the rest of the book? Why is it more like an episode out of *Tom Sawyer?*" Your answers to these questions and others like them are certain to have an argumentative edge.

Make a list of such questions.

3. Search for answers.

The literary selection itself should supply the answers. If at first you don't find them, search again. Think about all the parts and how they fit together.

4. Choose an answer.

The answer that you select should be the one that interests you the most and that you believe you can back up most convincingly with evidence *from the literary work itself.* This answer is your thesis.

It would be foolish to pretend that this process is easy. It isn't. It takes a great deal of close reading and a great deal of hard thinking. You will soon discover, however, that it's well worth the effort. Once you have established a firm thesis, half the battle of writing a literary paper is over. But even more important than this is the fact that the work of establishing a thesis has a way of opening your eyes to new ways of looking at literature, thus vastly enriching your ability to understand and interpret everything you read.

And that, of course, is what the study of literature is all about.

The Full Literary Thesis

The thesis of a literary paper seldom requires the full pro-and-con treatment. Your main purpose is to explore and explain, not to argue. Therefore, when you start putting together your full and final thesis, forget about the points that might be made against it. Simply list all the evidence you can find to support it.

That word *evidence* is important. It is not enough to say that you "feel" something to be true—that you feel, for example, that Hester Prynne is the strongest and most courageous character in *The Scarlet Letter*. You must find evidence in the work itself to back up such statements. Piece by piece, you must build up the case for your thesis.

As you locate each bit of evidence, make a note of it under your thesis. If your selection is a full book or a short story, jot down the page number where the evidence appears. If your selection is a poem, locate your evidence by stanza and line. This makes it easy to find the passage quickly when you need it and, if necessary, to quote it exactly.

Your list of evidence will serve as a guide when you write your paper. Number the items on your list in order of importance, and work your way through the list point by point, saving your most important piece of evidence until last. The result should be a clear, logical, well-organized literary paper.

Putting It All Together

Since you are not including con statements in your full thesis, you will not make the usual concessions to the opposition in the final paper. In all other respects, the structure of the literary paper will be like the structure of any other essay: introduction, middle section, conclusion. Follow the forms outlined in Figures 4 and 5 in Chapter 4, but omit the concessions.

Paragraph structure, of course, will follow the usual pattern: topic sentence, explanation and illustration, concluding sentence. The middle section, again, is where you build your case. It is in these middle paragraphs that you present the evidence you have gathered from the literary work to support the point you are making.

If you have set out to show, for example, that Mark Twain considered racial prejudice a great social evil and mounted a fierce attack upon it in *Huckleberry Finn*, you might come up with a paragraph like this:

> Twain establishes his position very early in the book in a key scene between Huck and his father. The older man has seen a black stranger in town and works

himself into a fury over the fact that the man is not only well dressed and well educated but is actually allowed to vote in his home state. He is outraged when he learns that a black man is protected for six months before he can be put up at auction and sold. It's a worthless "govment," he thinks, that must "set stock-still for six whole months before it can take a-hold of a prowling, thieving, infernal, white-shirted free nigger. . . ." This is the only scene in the book in which proslavery sentiment is openly and brutally expressed, and it is no accident that Mark Twain chose to put the words in the mouth of Huck's father. Finn is a drunkard, a liar, a thief, a child-beater, a completely ignorant and vicious man with no redeeming qualities whatever. Twain could hardly have expressed his contempt for proslavery views more effectively.

Once you have presented all your evidence, you are ready to conclude. Your final paragraph, shaped like a pyramid, will open with a sentence that echoes but does not repeat your thesis and will move gracefully to your closing statement.

Sometimes you are given a very specific literary topic to write about. You may even be given a thesis to defend or attack. In such instances you should be thankful. Part of your work has already been done for you. You have only to collect the evidence and write the essay. The form of the essay itself will be the same as the form you have been studying.

The Book Review

The book review is a formal essay similar to the literary paper. There are, however, differences. If the literary paper deals with a novel or short story, it is usually limited to some one aspect of that book or story. The book review, in contrast, concerns itself with the work as a whole.

The task of the reviewer is to demonstrate how successfully the book accomplishes what the author set out to do. That means that the reviewer must understand thoroughly what the author had in mind. The thesis of the review—and the review must have a thesis—is based upon an evaluation of the entire work.

You may sometimes be expected to review a book or a short story. The assignment may not come from an English class. It could be for social studies or science or almost any other course. Have no fear. You are ready for it. Your inventory is in the book, and your principal question is "What does this all add up to?" Take inventory and answer the question. When you have done that, you have all the material for your essay at hand. Proceed with confidence.

The Performance Review

The play or movie or dance or music review is similar to the book review. The thesis is based upon the work or the performance as a whole. Your central impression of the performance is your thesis. The chief difference is this: you see and listen to plays or movies or dance or music, rather than read them. (You would be wise to read a play, however, if that's possible, before you review it.) In terms of writing, your review follows the standard essay form: thesis and evidence supporting your thesis.

The Essay Test

The essay test is probably misnamed. In general, almost any test that requires a written statement of any kind as an answer is called an essay test. Rarely does it have anything to do with the essay as such. Nevertheless, your work with the essay will come in handy when you face the essay test.

Keep in mind that you should do precisely what the essay question asks you to do. If it asks you to describe something, describe it; if it asks you to explain something, explain it; if it says outline, then outline. And so on. Many students blunder on essay tests for the simple reason that they fail to heed the demands of the question.

Do what the question asks or tells you to do. The rest depends, first, upon your knowledge of the subject and, second, upon the skill you have developed in writing the paragraph. If the question calls for a simple statement of fact, by all means settle for that. But if it requires a more detailed response, put your skill with the paragraph to work. Each paragraph will be like a miniature essay with topic sentence, development of topic idea, and concluding statement. Your answer may require more than one paragraph. No problem. Just remember, only one point to each paragraph.

Summary

The literary paper is a common assignment in most English classes. In its longer form it is essentially a formal essay; in its shorter forms it corresponds usually to some part of an essay, such as a paragraph or two. It usually involves an interpretation of a literary work, and that interpretation can be stated as a thesis.

Related forms of the literary paper appear in the book review and in the play or movie review and similar critical writing. All these represent variations of the formal essay.

No one who has mastered the structure of the formal essay and the reasoning behind it, and who possesses the rudiments of style, need ever again be seriously troubled by any kind of writing assignment. Although the specific requirements of various kinds of papers may vary, the fundamentals remain the same: skill in organizing and skill in manipulating the sentence and the paragraph. Remember that, and you need never again turn pale at the prospect of any written exam or any required paper in any course you have truly studied.

You may, in fact, find yourself rather enjoying such a prospect. It happens.

QUESTIONS

1. In what ways does the literary paper resemble the formal essay?

2. What determines the way you would go about reading a given work of literature?
3. What would you be likely to include in your inventory of a poem?
4. Why do students often go astray when they take an essay test?

1. Find a good dictionary of literary terms in your library and look up the words *mood* and *tone*. What do they mean when they are applied to a work of literature? Explain in a paragraph how a work of literature might display a light mood but a deeply serious tone.
2. Read the two poems mentioned in this chapter: MacLeish's "Epistle to Be Left in the Earth," on pages 189–190, and Frost's "Stopping by Woods on a Snowy Evening." In two or three paragraphs (or as many as you need) describe the differences in form of the two poems. Include in your description a comment on Frost's method of connecting his stanzas.
3. Find a short poem or a short story that you like and write a review of it. Select one that has sufficient depth to make writing about it worthwhile. It should be one you have not studied in class.

VOCABULARY

Look up the following words in a dictionary. Write a paragraph about some aspect of writing in which you use correctly at least three of the words.

devastate	prevail (ing)	aimless
objective	epistle	enhance

14

Summing Up

All writing—not just the writing we classify as literature, but all writing, from the most ordinary to the most sublime—springs from the very simple and very basic urge of human beings to communicate with each other. You write for the same reason you talk: because you have something to say. Oddly, that large and obvious truth is often overlooked or forgotten. Yet nothing else is as important as this to writers who hope to improve their craft. The first principle of writing can be put into these four words: Have something to say.

That is where writing begins. And that is why so much of your early work in this book was with thesis and structure, with sifting and evaluating your ideas until you were certain of your own opinion on a subject, and then with developing that opinion into essay form. You learned, in short, to think before writing.

It was not easy work. Thinking is never easy. To many of you it must have seemed a slow, arduous, unglamorous, exasperating way of going about writing. But from that labor you should have emerged with something every writer must have: a sense of structure.

And then you were ready to pursue that elusive thing called "style."

No book, of course, could supply you with all the elements that go into a writer's style, for ultimately your style reflects everything that you are—your attitudes, your capacity for thought and feeling, the whole quality of your mind and imagination. A book can only point out those elements of style that are common to all good writing, explain some of the techniques that experienced writers use in the practice of their craft, and supply an assortment of guideposts, short-cuts, insights, advice, examples, and exercises—all designed to help you say what you want to say with precision and grace.

That is what this book has tried to do.

In the process, it has required you to work very hard. You have had to break old habits and establish new ones. You have analyzed and invented and listened and read and written and rewritten. Moving from whole essay to paragraph to sentence to single words, and then back to whole essay again, building paragraphs, experimenting with every kind of sentence, searching for *le mot juste,* trying your hand at unfamiliar techniques, you have written many thousands of words. It has been a long and rigorous apprenticeship.

And of course it is not finished. As long as you continue to write, you will continue to learn. But even now (if you have been a faithful apprentice up to this point) you should be able to see a great improvement in your own work. No matter what your writing was like before you started— whether it was very good or very bad—it should be better now. You certainly have the right to expect that.

You can also expect some very tangible benefits as a student. You can expect to perform now at a higher level on any kind of writing assignment. Essay questions on examinations should never again look quite so forbidding. Term papers should have lost some of their terrors. If you are a college student, or if you are college bound, a great deal of writing lies ahead of you. You are ready for it.

And you can expect one other benefit—one that will last a lifetime, no matter how you spend your future: you will be a better reader. You will be able to see almost immediately what other writers are trying to do, what points they particularly want to make, how they create their effects. You will know these things because, as the saying goes, you have been there yourself. You will be able to spot bad writing in an instant—you are likely, in fact, to become a quite deadly critic. But you will also delight in good writing, because you know how it got that way. It all adds up to greater pleasure in reading.

But most important of all will be your own sure sense that you can communicate with others through written words, can say what you mean and say it well. It is a fine and exciting thing to learn how to handle with skill and assurance that most marvelous and complex and magical instrument, the English language. For language is the most splendid achievement of civilized peoples and it is a powerful instrument indeed. Use it with pride.

Index

205

2 3 4 5 6 7 8 9 ◆ 85 84 83 82